A SYNTAX-ORIENTED TRANSLATOR

A SYNTAX-ORIENTED TRANSLATOR

SECOND PRINTING, REVISED

Peter Zilahy Ingerman

RADIO CORPORATION OF AMERICA
ELECTRONIC DATA PROCESSING
CHERRY HILL, NEW JERSEY

1966

ACADEMIC PRESS · New York and London

ACADEMIC PRESS INC.
111 Fifth Avenue, New York, New York 10003

United Kingdom Edition published by
ACADEMIC PRESS INC. (LONDON) LTD.
Berkeley Square House, London W.1

LIBRARY OF CONGRESS CATALOG CARD NUMBER: 66-14467

First Printing, 1966
Second Printing Revised, 1967

PRINTED IN THE UNITED STATES OF AMERICA

Preface

The purpose of this book is to present a single syntax-oriented translator. The reader is assumed to be familiar with the field of programming and to have some experience with the inner mysteries of compilers and translators, but not with syntax-oriented translators specifically. The patient reader will find the presentation of the translator sufficiently detailed for him to construct a copy for himself; hopefully, he will also be able to improve on it for his own purposes.

The book was originally intended for the home compiler-writer who had need of a syntax-oriented translator and found the literature vague, obfuscatory, and hubristic.

Since very few people write compilers at home, and not very many people know what syntax is, anyhow, the scope of the book has been broadened, thus making it vague, obfuscatory, and hubristic.

The fundamental approach taken is that of Irons [I6lc]; the translator is a bottom-up type, with separate parsing and unparsing. There are, however, a number of significant extensions which are incorporated, both with respect to the types of languages which are translatable and with respect to the types of target languages which may be generated.

A number of people have suffered beyond the call of duty in the preparation of this book. First is the author's wife who has valiantly removed semicolons, insisted on examples, and demanded that topic sentences be followed by paragraphs; the book owes its readability to her.

Others have worked through preliminary turgidity in order to clarify the author's intent (and in some cases his confusion). In lexicographical order particular mention must be made of Alonzo Grace, Jr., Marvin Graham, Mark Halpern, Nick Katz, Charles Kerpelman, Brian Randell, and George Shapiro.

Finally the author acknowledges his innate stubbornness and his consequent responsibility for all remaining errors, misstatements, and cases of "it is obvious . . . ."

The work reported herein has been performed part under Contract AF-49 (638)-1452 with the United States Air Force Office of Scientific Research of the Office of Aerospace Research: the work has also been supported in part by the Westinghouse Electric Corporation.

February 1966   PETER ZILAHY INGERMAN

Preface to the Second Printing, Revised

The revisions to this second printing comprise a number of typographical errors which have been found by G. Miller Clarke and Peter Shantz, together with some revisions of text and figures where the errors were too blatant to be left as exercises for the reader. Particular attention should be paid to pages 52 and 53, as well as to the diagrams of Chapter 4. These latter have been corrected so that backup now works.

A belated acknowledgment should be made to G. Miller Clarke, who redrew Fig. 3.14 for the first printing; the original was patterned after Medusa, and was overcryptic.

Finally, the author's wife has again jumped into the fey, with the consequence that the additions are more comprehensible than they otherwise would have been.

Contents

Glossary of Definitions

CHAPTER 1

Introduction and Definitions

Introduction—A General Description of a Problem

There are five general steps in the solution of a problem on a large-scale digital computer. Initially, someone must state that the problem exists. Next, the problem must be formulated in a careful and methodical way. This includes the requisite numerical analysis, a delineation of the gross logical elements of the problem, and an estimate of the quantity of data that will be required as source data or will be generated as result data. The usual result of the formulation is a set of process-charts, some text giving the analysis, and a general (but carefully written) summary of the problem.

The next three steps in the solution of a problem depend on a specific machine, to some extent. They are: restating the problem in terms of a particular computer (and, perhaps, in terms of a particular configuration of some computer); coding the problem for that computer, in a language which it will understand; and finally, executing the problem. The (perhaps greater) task of preparing the requisite input data for the problem has not been mentioned, nor has the (usually greater) problem of interpreting the results of the running of the problem.

Each of these five steps may fail, in the sense that the effect of attempting a step may result in reevaluating any or all of the previous steps. It is possible, for example, that a problem may become moot before it is well enough understood to formulate carefully.

With the early machines, all coding was done in machine language. For binary machines, this resulted in a plethora of ones and zeros; a

1

logical development was to write a program for the machine that would accept as input some sort of mnemonic language which could be translated (or, better, transliterated) by the machine itself, thus relieving the coder of the ones and zeros.

This transliteration program was called an *assembler*. It soon became obvious that the assembler could perform many other bookkeeping tasks for the programmer beyond that of mere transliteration. Addresses were written in decimal (rather than in octal or hexadecimal) notation; conversion to binary, being a purely algorismic process, was performed by the machine. In places where a reasonable set of standard assumptions saved the coder some drudgework, assumptions were made; it was no longer necessary to specify the location of each line of coding explicitly, but rather only when the line was to be placed in a location which was not the immediate (logical) successor of the preceding line of coding. The coder still wrote in a language isomorphic to machine code; the only change was in the specific characters which had to be written to effect the identical computation, and these (new) characters were chosen to make the task of the coder an easier one.

Such rudimentary routines actually existed. The next extension may be called the formal introduction of *automatic programming*. Automatic programming is defined by Carr [C59a] as "all those methods which attempt to shift the burden of formulation and programming for automatic computers onto the machines themselves". The main historical reason for the development of automatic programming techniques was to free the programmer from the repetitive (and error-fraught) portions of his job.

Early in the development of assembly routines, the notion of a *symbolic address* was introduced. A symbolic address was defined only by its appearance in appropriate places in the coding, and not by any relationship to the machine. Symbolic addresses freed the programmer from routine bookkeeping details. Further, correcting the symbolic form of the program was much simpler than correcting the machine-language coding, since the corrections had no incidental effect on the symbolic addresses as such, but only on the absolute (machine) addresses that were assigned by the assembly program on the next assembly.

Facilities for the automatic inclusion of previously written routines as *library routines* were also introduced into the primitive assembly program. Library routines relieved the programmer from the necessity of writing (or copying) the same lines of coding for certain common pro-cesses, wherever the need arose. Instead, he wrote an instruction *to* the assembly routine which requested the automatic inclusion of a specific program from the library, either by the assembler or at load time. Since there was no basic reason why *any* piece of coding could not be included in a library, libraries became rather large, and the task of finding an appropriate routine in the library began to be almost as time-consuming as rewriting the same routine would have been. On the other hand, various pieces of the assembly program itself could be included in the library, which made the creation of more sophisticated assembly systems considerably easier than the writing of their predecessors.

Assembly systems, although relieving the coder of much of the drudge-work, still did not eliminate the coder entirely. Problems still had to be coded in a machine-like language, and a skilled technician was required to perform this function.

The next step in the automation of coding was the one-to-many translation. Unlike an assembly system, where the translation was essentially one-to-one, the one-to-many translator allowed the coder to write his instructions in a sort of shorthand; the machine was made to translate this shorthand into its own machine-language instructions, and then to execute the instructions so generated. Two modes of performing this process arose: the interpretive mode, in which each instruction was translated and then immediately executed (in fact, the translation might be only implicit), and the translative mode, in which all of the translation took place, followed by the execution of the entire corpus of resulting machine instructions. The "pure" interpretive mode is now not generally used for those systems which demand running efficiency,* but is still widely used in experimental systems. On the other hand, the "pure" translative system also occurs only rarely, since many of the complex systems now being used require that the storage and other resources allocated for use by a specific program be determined at the time that program is executed. This results in (usually all of) the input and output instructions of the program being handled in an interpretive manner, although the remainder of the program may be translated.

At this stage in the development of automatic programming, it was recognized that a problem stated in a particular shorthand was not

---

* Although all machine languages are by definition interpreted by their machines and are hence an exception.

limited to a particular computer for solution; given appropriate translation (or interpretive) programs, the same shorthand could be read as input data by entirely different computers, translated into the machine code, and executed. Indeed there was no reason, because of the data-processing nature of the problem, why the translation could not take place on one machine and the actual execution take place on another. (However, it should be clear that the use of different machines obviates an interpretive mode except as mentioned at the end of the preceding paragraph.)

Recognition of the independence of language and machine spurred interest in languages designed for the users of computers, so that users could state problems in a language more natural to them than the shorthands mentioned in the preceding paragraph. In fact, such *procedure-oriented languages* attempted to free the problem analyzer from consideration of the machine on which his problem would be executed, thus leaving him free to consider only the procedure by which the problem was to be solved. Also, the problem analyzer was freed from the onerous task of communicating his problem to a person who was conversant with the programming of the machine on which the problem was to be solved, but perhaps not conversant with even the rudiments of the process used in solving the problem. The success of this idea may be measured (albeit crudely) by the proliferation of programs for various machines which translate into the corresponding machine languages from a rather small number of procedure-oriented languages. However, this very proliferation has introduced an additional problem—the expenditure of effort in writing the translation programs themselves. Although the requisite effort has become less as more experience has been gained, considerable study has been made of various techniques to make the task even easier.

One of the earliest techniques developed was called *bootstrapping*. Although developed early, it is elegant, still in use, and deserves mention. Initially, some simple assembly system is produced for a machine, frequently by coding directly in machine language. This rudimentary assembly system is then used to assemble a more sophisticated assembly system, and so on. Finally, a translator is produced which will translate some fairly simple procedure-oriented language into machine code. This translator is used to translate a more sophisticated translator, for a more sophisticated language, and so on.

Although bootstrapping reduces the programming effort required to produce translators for new languages, it requires a major investment of programmer time. Considerable study has therefore been made of the characteristics of procedure-oriented languages themselves, with an eye to the development of a technique for simplifying the translators which must be bootstrapped. The connection of such studies with the problem of translating from one natural language to another has been noted, and "programming languages" is less and less a misnomer and more and more a field of interest to linguists.

Definitions

There are various reasons for an author's including wholesale definitions at the beginning of a book, and it is only fair to admit that none of them bode well for the reader. However, in this field, as in all technical fields, there is a tendency for conventional words to be imbued with precise meanings which are occasionally different from (as well as more precise than) the intuitive meanings attributed casually to them. The terms that will be used in a specific technical sense are italicized at the point of their definition; for the benefit of the casual reader, a list of all such terms, together with references to their definitions, is given in a Glossary. A conscientious attempt has been made to avoid giving a technical meaning to a word which is in contradiction to its casual meaning. Hence, the reader who wishes to read on without remembering all of the definitions may do so without becoming totally lost, although he may expect his understanding to be lessened.

The definitions are given in narrative form; the definition is first stated and is then followed with an example, where needed. As a consequence, a definition may not be clear until the paragraph which it starts has been read. Finally, it must be pointed out that the goal of this set of definitions is the precise definition of the word "translator", as it is used in the title of this book.

An *object* is a mark which denotes itself or the class of marks similar to itself. When it is necessary to identify an object, it will be enclosed in quotation marks. Objects themselves will be printed in a boldface sans serif type. (Note that this definition, since it refers to *marks*, applies to objects which are written; obvious extensions to other types of communications can be made by replacing "marks" with "signals".)

The phrase "the class of marks similar to itself" in the definition of object may seem to be superfluous; an example will point out its necessity.

Consider the two separate statements:

$$\text{“}+\text{” is a plus sign.}$$
$$\text{“}+\text{” is not a plus sign.}$$

If the phrase in question were eliminated from the definition of object, both of these statements could be simultaneously true, since the object in the first statement is (a physically distinct and therefore) a different object from that which appears in the second statement. As the definition is given, however, one of the two statements is true and the other false, which is more natural.

Two manipulations may be made on objects: *juxtaposition* and *concatenation*. Juxtaposition of two objects means simply placing the objects together; one may say, therefore, juxtaposed on the right or juxtaposed on the left, indicating the relation of the second object to the first.* Juxtaposition may well change the spatial relationship between objects, but has no effect on the identifiability of the objects. As an example, if "**a**" and "**b**" are juxtaposed, the result is written "**a**""**b**", where each of the individual objects is surrounded by quotation marks to indicate its continuing individual identity.

Concatenation, on the other hand, involves not only a possible spatial rearrangement, but also the loss of identity on the part of the objects concatenated, together with the assumption of an identity on the part of the concatenation. To continue with the example of the preceding paragraph, if "**a**" and "**b**" were to be concatenated, the result would be "**ab**".

One further observation must be made with respect to juxtaposition and concatenation. Consider the set of objects

$$\{\mathbf{a, b, c, ab, bc}\}$$

Any juxtaposition of elements of this set, such as

$$\text{“ “ “a” ” “b” ” ” “c” ”}$$
$$\text{“a” “ “ “b” ” “c” ” ”}$$
$$\text{“ab” “ “c” ”}$$
$$\text{“a” “ “bc” ”}$$

---

* The definitions of juxtaposition and concatenation are quite general, and the restriction implied by "juxtaposition on the right" and "juxtaposition on the left" should be understood as one of convenience, not of necessity. The languages to be discussed in this book will be limited to *linear* languages; that is, languages which can be thought of as being written on a single, suitably long, line.

must by definition be uniquely dejuxtaposable, since the elements of the set do not lose their identity through juxtaposition. On the other hand, the concatenation

$$\text{``abc''}$$

is clearly not uniquely deconcatenable, since it could have been formed by concatenation of any of the objects juxtaposed above; after the concatenation is performed, only the result of the concatenation has an identity.

An important rule may now be given: *Any concatenation of objects is an object.* Some concatenations of objects may be more useful, or desirable, than others; for example, not all concatenations of letters of the alphabet form words in the dictionary. The juxtaposition of objects may (but need not) be considered as an object.

Finally, it must be pointed out that concatenation is associative but noncommutative, and juxtaposition is neither associative nor commutative. (Proof of the properties of concatenation is in [G59].) The proof that juxtaposition is noncommutative is left as an exercise; intuitively, it seems desirable that "a""b" and "b""a" be different. The non-associativity of juxtaposition is best illustrated by example: Consider the phrase "half baked chicken". Is the chicken half finished cooking, or is only half of a cooked chicken being discussed? Symbolically, there is a difference between

$$\text{`` `` h '' `` b '' '' `` c ''}$$

and

$$\text{`` h '' `` `` b '' `` c '' ''}$$

in which the parenthesization of the juxtapositions is made explicit by the additional quotation marks. (This example will be used again in Chapter 3, where juxtaposition and concatenation will be discussed in more detail.)

The explicit indication of the parenthesization of juxtapositions is frequently unnecessary when the grammar is sufficiently simple so that the intended grouping may be adduced from the objects that have been juxtaposed. Unfortunately, it is customary to omit the parenthesization even for non-trivial grammars, with the hope that the resulting confusion will be small.* An *accretion* is the result of juxtaposing an object with the result of a previous juxtaposition, but without indication of the parenthesi-

* It is usually not [L65].

zation. The juxtaposition of two accretions is also an accretion, as are (as special cases) a single object and the juxtaposition of two objects. A typical accretion is

hbc

where the parenthesization of the preceding example is not given.

Syntax may now be defined as the juxtaposition and concatenation of objects. A *rule of syntax* states some permissible (or prohibited) relation between objects; e.g. the juxtaposition **qq** never occurs in English. Finally, a *grammar* is a set of rules of syntax which define the permissible (in a descriptive grammar) or desired (in a prescriptive grammar) relations between objects. It is particularly important to note that a grammar gives no meaning to objects or sequences of objects; it merely forms the basis for determining whether an arbitrary sequence of objects is a member of the set of grammatical sequences.

Semantics is defined as the relationship between an object and the set of meanings attributed to the object. A *symbol* is an object to which at least one meaning has been attributed by a *rule of semantics*. Note that not all objects are symbols, and that concatenation of symbols yields a symbol only if an additional rule of semantics attributes a meaning to the newly formed object (since the elements of a concatenation lose their individual identities, *including* any attributed meanings). Juxtaposition of symbols may produce a new symbol, with a meaning (attributed by a rule of semantics) that is not apparent from the meanings of the con- stituent symbols. In natural languages, this phenomenon is called an *idiom*. In general, however, the juxtaposition of symbols produces a new symbol whose meanings are derivable from the meanings of the constituents.

There are concatenations of letters which are not words, and there are juxtapositions of words which are not sentences; the determination of "wordness" or "sentenceness" is completely independent of any semantics of either individual words or individual sentences. For example, **xtqk** is a perfectly good concatenation of letters, but is not a word; "ago computer which an to output" is not a sentence, although each of its constituents is a word. On the other hand, there are words which have no meaning in their own right ("it" is an example) and there are sentences which are meaningless, even though grammatical ("Taste the scrubbing sonata.").

Pragmatics is the relation between a symbol and its users. (An object must have at least one meaning attributed to it before it becomes pragmatically significant.) A *rule of pragmatics* is one which selects from among the set of meanings attributed to a symbol that particular meaning which is significant to a particular user at a particular time. As a rather simple example, consider the object " **H** " with the meanings "letter of the alphabet". In English-speaking countries, the sound associated with this symbol is the aspirated sound at the beginning of the word "hay". In Greek, this symbol denotes (approximately) the vowel sound at the end of the same word "hay". Finally, in Russian, the denoted sound is that associated in English with the letter "N". For a person who writes all three languages, the rule of pragmatics is the use of the language being written, and the significant meaning is obviously a function of time.

The word "meaning" has been used in the definition of both semantics and pragmatics. Its precise definition has been argued by philosophers, lawyers, theologians, and psychiatrists, and is beyond the scope of this book. None the less, an informal description may be of some use. A *denotation* is an explicit meaning, e.g. a dictionary definition of a word. A *connotation* is a suggested meaning, e.g. an apple denotes a particular kind of fruit, but may connote good health.* Denotations may be of two kinds, *public* and *private*. A public denotation is an explicit meaning which may be expected to be part of common knowledge. A private denotation, although still an explicit meaning, is common only to some small group (or even a single individual, although this is unlikely); argot, jargon, and slang are terms used to denote private denotations. Connotations are also public and private. When some specific denotation is determined, pragmatically, to be the significant meaning of a symbol, the other denotations may be considered as public connotations. (An overworked example of this is the word "bow".) A private connotation is a suggested (as contrasted with an explicit) meaning which is the "property" of some specific individual. When dealing with procedure-oriented languages, the private connotations and the public denotations may be considered non-existent, since the symbols in procedure-oriented languages are defined either by the programmer or the language specifier, and in either case are private denotations.

Unlike many of the words so far defined, "ambiguity" is adequately defined in the dictionary. The definition is included here for completeness:

* "An apple a day keeps the doctor away."

ambiguity—The quality or state of: having two or more possible meanings; being of uncertain signification; susceptible of different interpretations; hence, obscure; not clear; not definite; uncertain or vague [after W55].

Certain kinds of ambiguity, relating to syntax, semantics, and pragmatics, are of particular interest. Although each of these kinds of ambiguity represents an uncertainty or vagueness, the type of uncertainty is of significance, as well as the mere existence of the uncertainty.

A *syntactic ambiguity* (also called an *amphiboly*) exists in two cases:

i. An object which is the result of a concatenation is not uniquely deconcatenable, or
ii. There is more than one way, according to the grammar, of associating the juxtapositions contained in an accretion.

It is significant that a syntactic ambiguity may not affect the determination of meaning—an example from Dutch may be of interest. The letter-pair "ij" occurs frequently in Dutch (where it is considered as a single letter); an umlauted "y" ("ÿ") also occurs, but less frequently. The letter-pair "ij" and the "ÿ" look alike when written (as compared with being printed) and can be used interchangeably. In fact, the "ÿ" is exactly the result of failing to deconcatenate the written "i" from the following written "j". (In this respect, the script which causes the ambiguity is the conventional script as taught in the United States.) This particular amphiboly (of the first type) results in no confusion, at least to those familiar with the language. "Half baked chicken" is an example of the second kind of amphiboly.

An accretion has been defined as the extended juxtaposition of objects, with parenthesization omitted. This definition includes, as a special case, the extended juxtaposition of symbols (since any symbol is an object, although not all objects are symbols). Hence it is meaningful to refer to (certain) accretions as symbols, always remembering their possible syntactic ambiguity. As an example of the juxtaposition of two symbols to produce a symbol, consider the characteristic Germanic property of agglutination.*

Semantic ambiguity exists when a symbol has two or more meanings attributed to it; this is most often the case, in a natural language. This

---

* Der Untergrundbahnhofplatzzeitungsverkäufer.

kind of ambiguity is most frequently cited as responsible for much of the difficulty with the translation of natural languages on computers. The ubiquitous "bow" is again an example.

A *pragmatic ambiguity of the first kind* exists when, at the time the single meaning of a symbol or an accretion is required, there is no way of determining that single meaning. A *pragmatic ambiguity of the second kind* arises when, in the course of determining the single meaning of a symbol or an accretion (at some specific time), the criteria by which the single meaning is being selected from among the set of possible meanings are such that there are no meanings which satisfy the criteria; in this case the symbol becomes an object, its meaning null, and the situation pragmatically ambiguous.

It is not meaningful to talk of pragmatic ambiguity of the first kind unless there is a precursory semantic ambiguity. Conversely, if a symbol or an accretion has no semantic ambiguity, it is impossible for it to be pragmatically ambiguous of the first kind, although it may be pragmatically ambiguous of the second kind.

The syntax of an accretion considered as a symbol (special case—a single symbol) may be significant in the application of a rule of pragmatics, and hence in the elimination of a pragmatic ambiguity. The phrase "half baked chicken" from above is such a case; since a preferred grouping is not indicated, and since no additional information is available, the inability to select a single meaning results in a pragmatic ambiguity of the first kind.

A pragmatic ambiguity of the second kind is illustrated by the following situation: On opening the box containing a kit to be assembled, the enclosed instruction manual is found to pertain to a kit other than the one enclosed. The instruction manual is then pragmatically ambiguous of the second kind, since at the time a unique meaning is required, there are no meanings from which to choose; no meaning was required until the box was opened, however.

A *message* is a pragmatically unambiguous accretion. It is important to note that a message may be both (or either) syntactically ambiguous and semantically ambiguous. The determining factor is that at the time a single meaning is required, there is one and only one meaning available. In a natural language, sentences are usually the smallest accretions that may be considered messages; paragraphs, chapters, and books are also (possible) messages.

A *process* is any general transformation which may be performed on input data to produce output data; degenerate cases may not require input or not produce output. A *processor* is anything which performs such a transformation. There is nothing in these definitions which requires the output data from a processor to be related to its input data, although there is usually some relation. Also, a processor may be, for example, a computer executing a program or a human being following an instruction manual.

Finally, and at long last, a translator may be defined. A *translator* is a processor (in this book, usually embodied in a computer by means of a computer program) which accepts as input a message in one language and produces as output a message in another language, with the requirement that there must be one single common meaning of the two messages (at the time when a meaning is required). Both the input and output messages may have different syntax, semantics, and pragmatics. However, there must be at least one meaning which is common to the input message (considered as an accretion) and the output message (considered as an accretion), and the rules of pragmatics of the two languages must be such that the same one, and only one, of the common meanings is selected for the meaning of the messages in the two languages.

This definition of a translator is consistent with the function of the translation of procedure-oriented languages to machine code, and also to the translation from one natural language to another. As a more careful attempt is made to convey not only the specific denotation of some symbol, but also to convey in the target language all of the connotations of the symbol in the source language, the footnotes to the translation become bulkier than the translation itself.

A few more definitions are required. A *metalanguage* is a language which is used to talk about (in any way) a language. If some language L_1 is used only to talk about some other language L_2, then L_1 is being used as a *metalanguage over* L_2. One of the characteristics of natural languages is that they may be used as their own metalanguages; one may talk about English in English, French in French, etc. A language which may be used as its own metalanguage is said to be *unstratified*.

A metalanguage used for the purpose of specifying the syntax of a language will be called a *metasyntactic language*; similarly, specification of semantics and pragmatics of a language will be done in a *metasemantic language* and a *metapragmatic language*, respectively.

A Description of a Syntax-Oriented Translator

The classical steps of translation from source language to machine code are shown in Fig. 1.1. In many of the classical translators, the assembly language indicated in Fig. 1.1 was not explicitly available. Some such

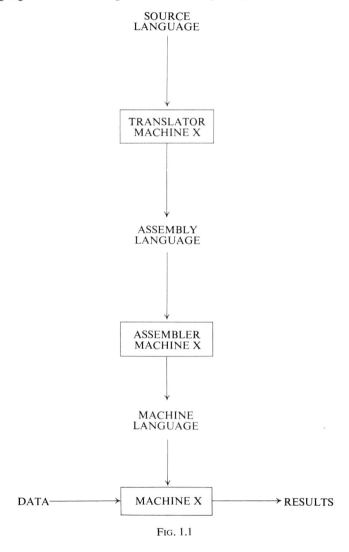

FIG. 1.1

translators did actually develop the equivalent of an assembly-language version of the program, but retained it in memory; others developed the assembly-language one instruction at a time and passed it on to an assembler in that form. However, all three of these configurations

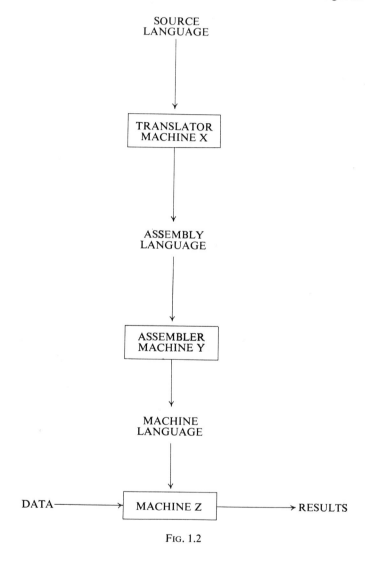

FIG. 1.2

(explicit-available, explicit-internal, and instruction-at-a-time) are considered to be exemplars of Fig. 1.1, in the sense that a clear distinction can be made between those functions which were part of translation and those functions which were relegated to the assembler. A few translators proceeded directly to machine code, without an intervening assembly step as defined above. This is considered as a degenerate case, and merely places the burden of the assembly functions in part on the translator itself and in part on the routine used to load the translated program into the memory for execution.

In Fig. 1.1, the translator runs on the same machine that the assembler runs on, and the machine language that is produced is also for the same machine. This is usually the case, but is a restriction of convenience, and not of necessity. In Fig. 1.2 the three different possible machines are indicated. It must be understood that a different machine may be either an entirely different machine or may be different configurations of the same machine.

The utility of more than one machine in this process was recognized early. Suppose that there exists for some machine P a procedure-oriented language in which a translation process can be specified. Call this language L. Suppose also that there is some machine Q for which there is no translator for the language L (and perhaps for no other languages, either). The following steps will bootstrap a translator for the language L onto machine Q:

   i. Write a translation program in L which specifies the translation from L to the language of machine Q.

  ii. Translate the program, using machine P. This produces a program which operates on machine P; this program will accept the language L and translate it into the machine language of machine Q.

 iii. Using the program generated at Step ii and operating on machine P, retranslate the translator which was written at Step i (whose first translation produced the program for machine P).

 iv. The result of this retranslation will be a program which will operate on machine Q, and which will accept programs written in language L and translate them into machine language for machine Q *using machine Q.*

Even the use of this technique (also called bootstrapping) does not appreciably diminish the programming effort required to make available a translator for a new language, particularly on a machine for which no other translators exist. The study of the linguistic properties of procedure-

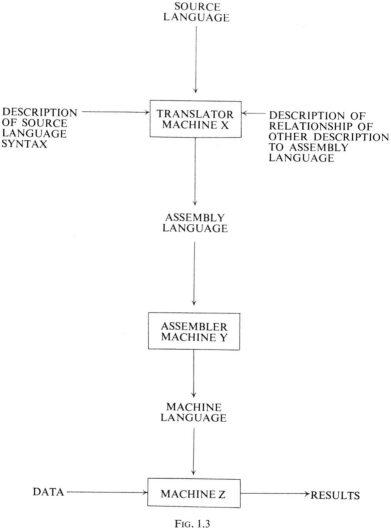

FIG. 1.3

oriented languages has led to the type of translator known as a *syntax-oriented translator*, which is diagrammed in Fig. 1.3. In contrast to Fig. 1.2, the translator has two additional inputs. These inputs are:

(a) A description of the source language syntax, written in a meta-syntactic language, and
(b) A description of the relationship between the description of the source language syntax and the assembly language itself.

Note that the second additional input defines the relationship between *another* description and a language. Such a description is in a meta-semantic and metapragmatic language.

This approach to the translation problem makes the translator independent of both the source and target languages. There is a dependence, however, on the form of the additional inputs. In other words, the translator is able to accept only source languages which may be described in the metalanguages which it is able to process; on the other hand, there is no inherent restriction to a single source language, but only to a class of source languages. As the metalanguages become more powerful, and the translator is modified to accept them, the class of translatable source languages increases.

There are several reasons for consideration of a syntax-oriented translator. A syntax-oriented translator can be used as a "compiler compiler". Because of the simplicity of the syntax-oriented translator, it is relatively easy to express it in a procedure-oriented language of the type translatable with the syntax-oriented translator; as a consequence, the bootstrapping to a new machine is not difficult. As a developmental tool, therefore, it allows the production of translators (and other types of software) for new computers with a small programming cost.

Some Comparisons and Comments

The writer of the classical translator, as portrayed in either Fig. 1.1 or 1.2, was aware, to some extent, of the syntactic properties of the source language. However, this awareness usually manifested itself in the writing of *generators*, each one of which was responsible for the production of the assembly language coding for a given entity from the source language. For example, a given generator was usually associated with the generation of coding for arithmetic expressions, while yet another might be invoked if a transfer-of-control statement (in the source language) were encountered. Each of these generators could be rather efficient, since it had only a single job to perform. The specific generators that were to be used were selected by an *analyzer*. In many cases, the analyzer and the generators are interlocked, and not easily separable.

For the classical translator, changes in the source language required as a minimum the changing of the analyzer, and quite possibly the addition or change of generators. This opened the door to the propagation of errors because of some unrecognized (by the changer) interdependence of the analyzer and the specific generators.

A change of target machine (or, less drastically, a change of assembly language) was also effected by changing all of the generators. At the expense of many table-look-ups at translation time, the specific sequences of assembly language coding produced by each generator were placed in a table, thus enabling a change of target machine by changing tables. Although this technique does tend to introduce fewer errors when changing target languages than changing the generators *per se*, a major problem still exists: The source language is also subject to change. Minor changes in the source language might be effected by relatively simple changes and additions to the generators (with corresponding changes in the table of assembly language coding), but a major change in the source language was likely to require an entire rewrite. If the two source languages had enough features in common, it was possible to use parts of the first translator as building blocks for the second, but a large-scale programming effort was still required.

The properties of the classical translator may be summarized as follows. It is comparatively efficient, in the sense that any desired balance between fast translation and fast machine code may be achieved. On the other hand, maintaining the translator, in the sense of incorporation of change or change of balance between translation time and running time, is at best a tedious job for a growing language; at worst, each change that is made in the translator can introduce new errors, which must then be located and eliminated. Finally, the production of a new translator, either for a new language or on a new machine (or both) can make at best limited use of the old.

The syntax-oriented translator is independent of the particular source language to be translated; rather, any language may be a source language, provided only that the metalanguages available for the auxiliary inputs to the translator are sufficient to describe the required properties of the desired language. The price that is paid is some inefficiency at translation time. However, a given set of tables will cause the syntax-oriented translator to have a specific balance between translation time and run time; as the tables get more detailed, and hence longer (for a specific language), the translation time increases, but the efficiency of the running code tends to increase as well. Since changing tables is a relatively simple process, a specific translator can be used to achieve any desired balance between translation time and running time, for any specific problem.

In contrast to the classical translator, change of assembly language or target machine requires only that the relationship between the description of the source language and the assembly language be redescribed; this description is exactly the right-hand of the additional inputs in Fig. 1.3. If the source language is changed or modified, both the additional inputs of Fig. 1.3 must be modified or changed. However, these inputs are in tabular form, and the interaction between changes is more readily discernible than in the classical case.

One of the most significant advantages of the syntax-oriented translator is its usefulness as a research tool. Because of the tabular structure of the additional inputs, there is no reason why an entire language (e.g. all of Algol-60 [N60] [N63]) must be presented; tables could well be written to translate only particular features of the language concerning which detailed studies were to be made. Statistics can be gathered on the use of particular language features, and the savings resulting from the testing for special cases (if any exist) can be found. Finally, as new languages are developed, they can be implemented piecemeal, and improvements to the language can be embodied as soon as they are specified, rather than when sufficient of them accumulate to warrant the risk of introducing errors into an already working system for the sake of the improved language.

A Short Bibliography

Since this first chapter is intended as an introduction, it seems appropriate to suggest some additional sources for "ancient history". A degenerate and elementary loading routine, but one which does do conversion from mnemonic instruction codes, is given in [I53], starting on page 81. Loading routines which divide the input of a program into small, individually correctable segments are discussed in [R53a], [L53], and [R56].

Elementary assembly systems are discussed in [R56a]; the addition of library facilities is mentioned in [G57], [R53], and [H60]. A one-to-many translator of an early type is discussed in [R55]; interpreters are discussed in [M60], [N60a], and [N60b]. Translators which were closer to processing problem-oriented languages are [P57] and [R60]. An introduction to one of the most widely known problem-oriented languages, one that is still having *ad hoc* translators written for it, can be found in either [C62] or [M61].

For general surveys of the history of automatic programming and of computer development, see [C59a], [G55], or [A58]. This last reference is predominantly concerned with hardware developments, but touches on programming.

CHAPTER 2

A Simple Language for
Some Simple Examples

The first chapter of this book concerned itself with a careful definition of the words used in the book's title, and closed with a very general picture of a syntax-oriented translator. This chapter is designed as a framework for the details of the remaining chapters. The metalanguages and processors to be discussed in later chapters are presented here in a strictly informal manner; unlike Chapter 1, the casual reader who assumes knowledge of the contents of this chapter will find little succor in the sequelae.

The Language of Simple Assignment Statements*

An *assignment statement* is a message whose meaning is that some variable is to assume a specified value; the specified value is usually the result of evaluating some arithmetic expression. A simple assignment statement, for the purpose of this chapter, is one in which the arithmetic expressions are restricted to extended additions and the number of different variables is small, say five. Such a simple assignment statement is constructed according to the three-rule grammar:

    i. Any of the objects **A**, **B**, **C**, **D**, or **E** will be considered to (2.0.1)
      be variables

---

* The author recognizes as valid the criticisms of papers in this field for the use of arithmetic expressions in any guise as the examples for compilation techniques. His excuse is that their simplicity, for this chapter, avoids the problem of the details obscuring the other points that are to be made. Later chapters will introduce less obvious problems.

    ii. An expression will be considered to be either a single   (2.0.2)
variable or an arbitrary number of variables separated
from each other by the object "**+**"

   iii. A simple assignment statement will be considered to be a   (2.0.3)
variable followed by the object "**=**" followed by an
expression.

Examples of simple assignment statements according to this grammar
are:

$$\textbf{A} = \textbf{A}$$
$$\textbf{B} = \textbf{C}$$
$$\textbf{A} = \textbf{B} + \textbf{C} + \textbf{E}$$

For a language as simple as this one, the natural-language form of the
grammar is sufficiently precise; for more complicated languages, a more
formal metasyntactic language is desirable to avoid misinterpretation of
the grammar (as well as to avoid amphibolous accretions). In the metasyntactic language to be used in this book, a *rule* has the general form of
an accretion of *metacomponents*, to the right of which is juxtaposed a
metaresult. As an example, consider the rule

$$\textbf{ABC} \langle d \rangle \qquad\qquad (2.1)$$

which is to be read "the object **A** followed by the object **B** followed by
the object **C** is given the name $\langle d \rangle$". The broken brackets are here used
to distinguish something which is to be considered the *name* of something
else. These names may also appear as metacomponents, as in the rule

$$\langle p \rangle \, \textbf{Q} \, \langle r \rangle \qquad\qquad (2.2)$$

which is to be read "something whose name is $\langle p \rangle$ followed by the
object **Q** is given the name $\langle r \rangle$". In order to determine whether a given
accretion (whose rightmost object must clearly be a **Q**) is to be given the
name $\langle r \rangle$, it is first necessary to determine whether the accretion that
remains after this rightmost **Q** has been dejuxtaposed may be given the
name $\langle p \rangle$. (This suggests, and correctly, that the use of a given rule of a
grammar may be contingent on the prior use of some other rule; 2.0.3
cannot be applied without both 2.0.1 and 2.0.2.)

    The grammar of simple assignment statements, using this formal metasyntactic language rather than the informal natural language of 2.0.1, 2.0.2, and 2.0.3, is:

$$\begin{aligned}
&\textbf{A } \langle\text{variable}\rangle && (2.3)\\
&\textbf{B } \langle\text{variable}\rangle\\
&\textbf{C } \langle\text{variable}\rangle\\
&\textbf{D } \langle\text{variable}\rangle\\
&\textbf{E } \langle\text{variable}\rangle\\
&\langle\text{variable}\rangle\ \langle\text{expression}\rangle && (2.4)\\
&\langle\text{expression}\rangle + \langle\text{variable}\rangle\ \langle\text{expression}\rangle\\
&\langle\text{variable}\rangle = \langle\text{expression}\rangle\ \langle\text{statement}\rangle && (2.5)
\end{aligned}$$

The five rules 2.3 correspond to the first informal rule 2.0.1, the two rules 2.4 to 2.0.2, and the last rule 2.5 to 2.0.3.

A grammar of a language, written in this formal metasyntactic language, constitutes the "description of the source language syntax" which is required as the first of the two additional inputs to the syntax-oriented translator of Fig. 1.3, and is used to control the parsing of the input accretion to determine whether or not it is grammatical. The purpose of the parsing processor is to provide to the second processor of the syntax-oriented translator a complete description (according to the grammar) of the interrelationships of all of the objects in the input accretion. These interrelationships, as well as the objects themselves, are used, in the second process, to determine the set of meanings which may be attributed to the objects to make them symbols, and to determine which particular meaning is to be selected by the rules of pragmatics. The second process will be discussed later in this chapter.

A form of parsing that is particularly convenient for human beings is *diagramming*; as an illustration, the parsing of the simple assignment statement:

$$\textbf{A} = \textbf{B} + \textbf{C} + \textbf{D} \qquad\qquad (2.6)$$

according to the grammar of 2.3, 2.4, and 2.5 is given by diagram 2.7 on the following page.

With the exception of the *head* of the tree (which is written at the top of the diagram*), every name (enclosed in broken brackets) is both a metaresult (as seen looking up the tree) and a metacomponent (as seen looking down the tree). Since objects are asserted but not defined, they

---

* Also known as the *root*, when it is written at the bottom [P37].

can appear only as metacomponents; on the other hand, the *head of the language* is defined as the name which appears at the head of the tree, and which otherwise must not be used.

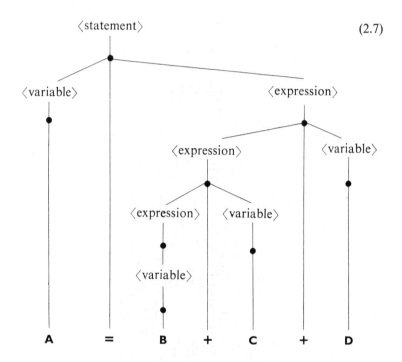

(2.7)

The rules of a language, then, form the first of the two additional inputs which distinguish Fig. 1.2 from 1.3, and also (in part) distinguish a conventional translator from a syntax-oriented one. In Fig. 1.3 there is a second additional input. This second input is a description of the relationship between the description of the source language syntax and the target assembly language, and provides the link between the parsing of the input accretion and the objects which are to be juxtaposed to form the output accretion. A way of doing this which emphasizes the rule-by-rule relationship is to associate with each rule of syntax an indication of the objects which should be included in the output accretion if the rule is used in parsing the input accretion. These indicata will be called *constructs*, and will usually be written following the rule with which they are associated. These constructs form the second additional input to the syntax-oriented translator of Fig. 1.3.

The grammar of simple assignment statements, but with the constructs shown, is:

$$\textbf{A} \langle\text{variable}\rangle \ \{\textbf{A}\} \qquad\qquad\qquad\qquad (2.8)$$
$$\textbf{B} \langle\text{variable}\rangle \ \{\textbf{B}\}$$
$$\textbf{C} \langle\text{variable}\rangle \ \{\textbf{C}\}$$
$$\textbf{D} \langle\text{variable}\rangle \ \{\textbf{D}\}$$
$$\textbf{E} \langle\text{variable}\rangle \ \{\textbf{E}\}$$
$$\langle\text{variable}\rangle \ \langle\text{expression}\rangle \ \{\textbf{L}[1]\}$$
$$\langle\text{expression}\rangle \ \textbf{+} \ \langle\text{variable}\rangle \ \langle\text{expression}\rangle \ \{[2]\textbf{A}[1]\}$$
$$\langle\text{variable}\rangle \ \textbf{=} \ \langle\text{expression}\rangle \ \langle\text{statement}\rangle \ \{[1]\textbf{S}[2]\}$$

The names appearing in a rule are numbered from right to left, starting with the metaresult being numbered 0; in the last rule of 2.8, "$\langle\text{variable}\rangle$" is numbered 2. (The = is unnumbered, since it is not a name.) The digits enclosed in the brackets "[" and "]" are interpreted as referring to a name *as a metacomponent*; the bracketed digit is to be replaced with the construct associated with the rule *of which that name is the metaresult*, according to the use of the rules in the parsing tree of some particular accretion.

The constructs of 2.8 assume a target assembly language containing the three mnemonic operation codes:

L   m   Load the accumulator with the contents of memory   (2.8.1)
                  location m

A   m   Add the contents of memory location m to the contents of the accumulator, placing the sum back into the accumulator

S   m   Store the contents of the accumulator in memory location m.

With these interpretations for the operations "**L**", "**A**", and "**S**", the rule and construct

$$\langle\text{variable}\rangle \ \langle\text{expression}\rangle \ \{\textbf{L}[1]\}$$

can be given the interpretation "under the assumptions that the object denoted by $\langle\text{variable}\rangle$ was known and had had a value assigned to it, then, *at the time the generated coding is executed*, load the accumulator with the value of that variable". The construct associated with this rule, then, generates coding such that when a variable becomes an expression, the corresponding behavior, *at the time the generated coding is executed*, is to place a value in the accumulator. If such a property of expressions is inheritable, then all expressions, regardless of the place where they appear on the parsing tree, can be assumed to have such a property. The second rule defining expressions, together with its associated construct, is:

$$\langle expression \rangle + \langle variable \rangle \langle expression \rangle \ \{[2]\mathbf{A}[1]\}$$

Under the assumption that an expression leaves (on execution) a value in the accumulator, this recursive definition of an expression generates coding which, when executed, adds to the accumulator the value associated with the variable and leaves the result of the addition in the accumulator as an expression. This particular construct, therefore, causes the desired inheritance of the property "the value of an expression, when the coding which evaluates it is executed, is in the accumulator".

The reader should perform the simple operation of verifying the construct associated with the final rule of 2.8. In particular, the relationship of the inheritable property of expressions with respect to statements should be understood.

An Example of Unparsing

Figure 2.7 showed the parsing of the simple assignment statement of 2.6 in accordance with the grammar of 2.3, 2.4, and 2.5. Once the input accretion has been parsed, it is necessary to unparse it by following through the constructs associated with the rules used in parsing.

In Fig. 2.7 the rules are indicated by dots. Figure 2.9 is the tree of constructs that results from associating with each rule its construct, and then connecting the constructs by drawing lines between the bracketed

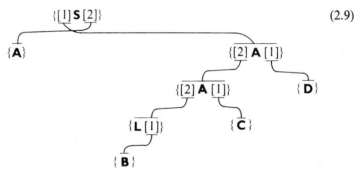

(2.9)

digits and the constructs to which they refer. The result of unwinding this tree of Fig. 2.9 is the accretion

$$\textbf{L B A C A D S A} \tag{2.10}$$

which, in a displayed (and more reasonable) format gives

$$
\begin{array}{ll}
\textbf{L} & \textbf{B} \\
\textbf{A} & \textbf{C} \\
\textbf{A} & \textbf{D} \\
\textbf{S} & \textbf{A}
\end{array}
\tag{2.11}
$$

This is exactly the coding (in the language of 2.8.1) that would be expected, given 2.6 as the input accretion.

Again, the reader should be sure that he understands the derivation of Fig. 2.9 from Fig. 2.7, and the generation of 2.10 from Fig. 2.9.

The Basic Translation Process

The basic translation process consists of two complementary processes: *parsing* and *unparsing*. The source language, considered as a string of objects, is parsed according to the grammar which is provided as the description of the source language in Fig. 1.3. If the source language input is ascertained to be grammatical, the parsing is completed, and a description of the rules used in the parsing process, the place in the parsing where they were used, and the constructs associated with them is made available to the unparsing processor. (If the input accretion is ungrammatical, some suitable indication may be given. This is in general a function of the particular implementation of the parsing processor, and is therefore beyond the scope of this book.)

Chapters 3, 4, and 5 of this book consider the metasyntactic language and the parsing in detail.

The unparsing process (which is fundamentally an interpretive process operating on the constructs in a sequence predicated on how the rules with which the constructs were associated were used in the parsing) generates as output the assembly language of Fig. 1.3. This assembly language is then processed to produce machine coding.

The constructs are expressed in a mixed metasemantic-metapragmatic language which is discussed in Chapter 6. Chapter 7 gives the details of the unparsing processor itself.

CHAPTER 3

The Metasyntactic Language

This chapter introduces the metasyntactic language that will be used to specify the grammars of the various source languages for the syntax-oriented translator. The notation is based on that suggested for the international algebraic language Algol [B60b] [N60] [N63].

The Metasyntactic Language in General

In Chapter 1 an object was defined as a mark which denoted itself or the class of marks similar to itself, and it was observed that the concatenation of objects was an object. It is convenient to have a special designation for an object which is not (or is not considered to be) the concatenation of other objects; such an object will be called a *base object*. As an example, the letters of the alphabet might be considered as base objects on a character-addressable computer, even though the machine representation of these characters required seven or eight bits.

Assume an ordered set **B** of base objects:

$$\mathbf{B} = \{\mathbf{b}_1, \mathbf{b}_2, \ldots, \mathbf{b}_m\} \tag{3.1}$$

In particular, $\mathbf{b}_1$ will be used to denote the null string. Also, assume an ordered set N of names:

$$N = \{n_1, n_2, \ldots, n_p\} \tag{3.2}$$

where elements of N are defined as being metalinguistic variables whose values are base objects or accretions of base objects. (This is the same sense in which "name" was used in Chapter 2.) In general an n_i may have as its values any of several different accretions of base objects, but n_1 is

29

defined as the unique name whose value is b_1 and only b_1.* Finally, for convenience, define the ordered set P:

$$P = \mathbf{B} \cup N - \{b_1\} = \{b_2, \ldots, b_m, n_1, \ldots, n_p\} \qquad (3.3)$$

It is required that juxtapositions of elements of P be uniquely dejuxtaposable into the constituent elements of P which form them; this is the reason for excluding b_1 from P. This requirement is placed on P so that the elements of the set E (to be defined in the next paragraph) will be unique.

Define the set E of extensions by the recursive relationship:

i. Every element of P is an element of E.

ii. If e_i and e_j are elements of E, then e_i juxtaposed with e_j is an element of E.

In other words, E is composed of all accretions of all lengths of elements of the set P. Although this produces an infinite set, no difficulty is encountered, since the set E is used as a conceptual tool only. If the requirement of the preceding paragraph on the unique dejuxtaposability of accretions into elements of P were not met, Rule ii for the formation of elements of E could lead to amphibolies of the first kind (illustrated in Chapter 1 by "ij").

The set R of *rules* may now be defined:

i. n_1 is an element of R. $\qquad\qquad\qquad\qquad\qquad\qquad\qquad$ (3.4)

ii. $e_i n_j$ is an element of R if $j \neq 1$. $\qquad\qquad\qquad\qquad\qquad$ (3.5)

The statements 3.4 and 3.5, together with $\mathbf{B}$ and N, give an effective definition of the set of rules.†

The element of E which enters into the definition of a rule (in 3.5)

---

* It may be well to consider the distinction between the null string, the object denoting the null string, and the name of the null string. In this book they are respectively

    (a)

    (b) b_1

and (c) n_1

If this does not clarify the point, the reader may well consider the White Knight's Song [C60b], [N56a].

† The notation of the Algol report [N60] [N63] is different, but obviously ancestral. In the first place, the element of N appearing explicitly in 3.5 was written on the left, rather than on the right, and was separated from the element of E by the symbol

is an accretion of elements of P, by the definition of the construction of the elements of the set E. These elements of P forming the element of E which appears in a rule will be referred to as the *metacomponents* of the corresponding rule; the element of N which appears to the right of the element of E in any element of R will be referred to as the *meta-result*. The prefix "meta" is applied to both these terms because they represent components and results in the metalanguage, rather than in the language specified by the metalanguage.

An Example of a Simple Language

The sets **B**, N, P, E, and R of the preceding section were defined independently of a language. In this section the syntax of a language of "assignment statements" (which are more complicated than the simple assignment statements of Chapter 2) will be specified. The five sets of the preceding section, when defined with respect to some language L, will be denoted by **B**(L), N(L), P(L), E(L), and R(L). (These may be read "the base objects of L", etc.)

In general, in the remainder of this book, sans-serif letters will be used for elements of **B**(L) and ordinary letters for elements of N(L). It may occasionally be convenient to identify an element of N(L) by enclosing it in the brackets "$\langle$" and "$\rangle$", as was done in the preceding chapter. Hence, "**A**" is an element of **B**(L), but "a", "$\langle A \rangle$", and "$\langle a \rangle$" are all (potentially) different elements of N(L). This is equivalent to requiring that **B**(L) $\cap$ N(L) equal the null set.

The sets **B**(L) and N(L), for the language of assignment statements, are:

$$\mathbf{B}(L) = \{\mathsf{A,B,C,D,E,F,G,H,I,J,K,L,M,N,O,P,Q,R,S,T,} \quad (3.6)$$
$$\mathsf{U,V,W,X,Y,Z,0,1,2,3,4,5,6,7,8,9,-,+,*,/,_{10},\cdot,(,}$$
$$\mathsf{),\uparrow,=\}}$$

"::=". In addition, a notational shorthand was introduced: Any subset of R of the form

$$\{n_i ::= e_{s_1} \quad n_i ::= e_{s_2} \quad ... \quad n_i ::= e_{s_n}\}$$

could be rewritten in the special form

$$n_i ::= e_{s_1}|e_{s_2}|...|e_{s_n}$$

The symbol "::=" is read "names the string"; the shorthand has the effect of introducing the symbol "|" into the metalanguage, with the reading of "or the string". See also [166].

$$N(L) = \{\text{adding operator, arithmetic expression,} \qquad (3.7)$$
$$\text{assignment statement, decimal fraction,}$$
$$\text{decimal number, digit, exponent part, factor,}$$
$$\text{identifier, integer, letter, left part, left part list,}$$
$$\text{multiplication operator, primary, term,}$$
$$\text{unary arithmetic expression, unsigned integer,}$$
$$\text{unsigned number}\}$$

(Note that 3.6 and 3.7 obey the notational convention of the preceding paragraph.) Since the elements of N(L) are metasyntactic variables whose values are accretions of elements of **B**(L), the significance of an element of N(L) is determined only by the rules of R(L), and not by the particular characters used. It is more convenient to use (physically) shorter symbols; mnemonic choice are the acronyms derived from 3.7, with some adjustment made for "identifier" and "integer":

$$N(L) = \{\text{ao,ae,as,df,dn,d,ep,f,id,in,l,lp,lpl,mo,p,t,uae,ui,un}\} \quad (3.8)$$

A	1	[1]	X	1		[24]		df	dn		[47]
B	1	[2]	Y	1		[25]		dn	ep	un	[48]
C	1	[3]	Z	1		[36]		dn	un		[49]
D	1	[4]	0	d		[27]		d	ui		[50]
E	1	[5]	1	d		[28]		ep	un		[51]
F	1	[6]	2	d		[29]		f	↑	p f	[52]
G	1	[7]	3	d		[30]		f	t		[53]
H	1	[8]	4	d		[31]		id	=	lp	[54]
I	1	[9]	5	d		[32]		id	l	id	[55]
J	1	[10]	6	d		[33]		id	p		[56]
K	1	[11]	7	d		[34]		l	id		[57]
L	1	[12]	8	d		[35]		lp	lpl		[58]
M	1	[13]	9	d		[36]		lpl	lp	lpl	[59]
N	1	[14]	−	ao		[37]		lpl	ae	as	[60]
O	1	[15]	+	ao		[38]		p	f		[61]
P	1	[16]	*	mo		[39]		t	mo	f t	[62]
Q	1	[17]	/	mo		[40]		t	ae		[63]
R	1	[18]	10	in	ep	[41]		uae	ae		[64]
S	1	[19]	.	ui	df	[42]		un	p		[65]
T	1	[20]	(	ae	) p	[43]		ui	d	ui	[66]
U	1	[21]	ao	t	uae	[44]		ui	df	dn	[67]
V	1	[22]	ao	ui	in	[45]		ui	dn		[68]
W	1	[23]	ae	uae	ae	[46]		ui	in		[69]

FIG. 3.9. R(L) for the language of assignment statements.

Figure 3.9 gives the set R(L) which specifies the syntax of the language of assignment statements. The elements of **B**(L) are, of course, those of 3.6, and the mnemonics of 3.8 have been used for the elements of N(L). Finally, each rule is suffixed by a rule number enclosed in brackets.

A Pictorial Representation of R(L)

An element of the set R(L) may be considered as a little piece of a directed graph. Consider the 62nd rule from Fig. 3.9; it is "t mo f t". Using the symbol "$\oplus$" to represent juxtaposition, this rule may be written in the form of a small directed graph:

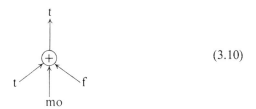

(3.10)

which may be further compressed to:

(3.11)

which shows the loop explicitly.

The other rule of R(L) from Fig. 3.9 which defines a "t" is the 53rd, which may be written:

$$t \\ \uparrow \\ f$$

(3.12)

No juxtaposition node is required, since this rule (and, in fact, all rules with only a single metacomponent) is construed as a renaming.

Using the symbol "$\widehat{V}$" to indicate a selection from among alternatives, the two pictures 3.11 and 3.12 may be combined to yield:

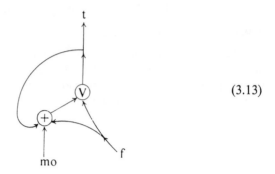

(3.13)

The entire set of rules of a language can be combined into a "graph of the language"; for the set of rules of Fig. 3.9, the graph of the language is given in Fig. 3.14. The graph of a language may have loops in it, but each rule appears only once. The diagram representing the parsing of a particular accretion (e.g. 2.7) has no loops, but rules may occur more than once or not at all, as dictated by the construction of the accretion. The repeated use of a rule or sequence of rules in parsing a particular accretion is equivalent to repeated traversing of a loop in the graph of the language.

Some Conditions on R

The kind of specification that has been given so far for the meta-syntactic language is a *generative* one; given the sets **B** and N, a sequence of manipulations is specified which will produce the infinite set R. Infinite sets are awkward when dealing with "practical" languages, and a *recognitive* approach avoids this difficulty. With a recognitive approach, a finite subset of R is presented, and the question asked: Is this subset of R an R(L) for some L?. Given an affirmative answer to this question, the additional question may be asked: What are the sets **B**(L), N(L), and P(L)?.*

---

 * The set E was generated so that all possible rules would be created from the sets **B** and N. Given a finite R(L), the only meaningful definition for E(L) is that an accretion of elements of P(L) is an element of E(L) only if it appears as the list of metacomponents in some rule of R(L). Hence, the set E(L) is considerably less important than the sets **B**(L), N(L), and P(L), given the set R(L).

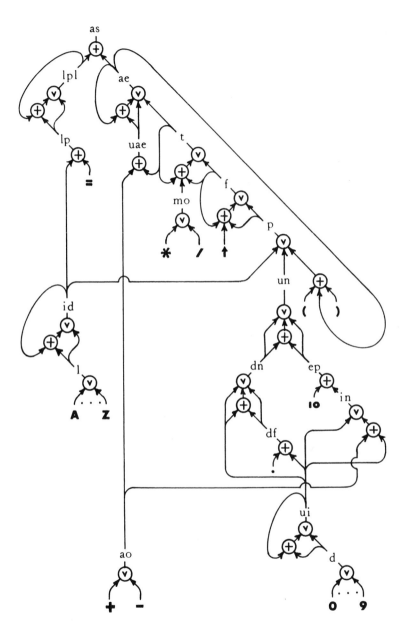

F<small>IG</small>. 3.14

This section states the conditions that must be met so that a subset of R will be an R(L) for some L. Some of these conditions are also amenable to a graphical interpretation, and Fig. 3.9 will be used as an example for this purpose.

The first condition that will be placed on R(L) is that it be *enterable*; an enterable set of rules is one such that each element of N(L) has at least one accretion of **B**(L) as its value, according to the rules R(L). Graphically, only an element of **B**(L) may label a branch which does not come from a node of some kind.

Given that the set R(L) is enterable, a useful pragmatic definition of P(L), **B**(L), and N(L) results. First, P(L) consists of anything that appears in R(L) as a metacomponent or metaresult, with the possible exception of b_1 (the null string). The set **B**(L) consists of those elements of P(L) (with the possible addition of b_1) that appear in R(L) as metacomponents and not as metaresults. Finally, N(L) contains all those elements of P(L) that are not elements of **B**(L). The condition of enterability is hence somewhat stronger than the condition that **B**(L) ∩ N(L) equal the null set, since it also provides an effective way of separating P(L) into N(L) and **B**(L).

The *heads of a language* are defined as those elements of N(L) which appear in R(L) as metaresults and not as metacomponents. The second condition that will be placed on a set R(L) is that it be *single-headed*; that is, that there be exactly one element of N(L) which is not used as a metacomponent. Graphically, all of the subtrees corresponding to individual rules must connect together, and there must be only one arrowhead which does not point to a node of some kind. This is a condition which does not restrict the class of languages which can be specified in the metasyntactic language, since many-headed languages can be made single-headed by the addition of rules which rename the multiple heads in terms of a new single head. By the pragmatic rules for determining the elements of N(L), these elements of N(L) which have been renamed cease to be heads of the language, since they now appear as metacomponents of the newly introduced rules.

A *grammatical source-language accretion* (which may or may not be a message!) may now be defined as an accretion of elements of **B**(L) which, through application of the rules R(L), may be recognized as having the name n_L, which element of N(L) is the single head of the language L.

Loops in the graph of a language have already been mentioned; a nonpictorial definition can be given. A *rule-chain* is a sequence of rules such that the metaresult of the kth rule is one of the metacomponents (or the sole metacomponent) of the $(k+1)^{st}$ rule. A single rule is a special case of a rule-chain. An illustration is given by:

$$e_{c_1} n_{r_1}, \ldots n_{r_1} \ldots n_{r_2}, \ldots n_{r_2} \ldots n_{r_3}, \ldots n_{r_3} \ldots n_{r_4} \qquad (3.15)$$

$$\underbrace{\phantom{e_{c_1} n_{r_1}}}_{r_1} \underbrace{\phantom{\ldots n_{r_1} \ldots n_{r_2}}}_{r_2} \underbrace{\phantom{\ldots n_{r_2} \ldots n_{r_3}}}_{r_3} \underbrace{\phantom{\ldots n_{r_3} \ldots n_{r_4}}}_{r_4}$$

Only the left-most rule of a rule-chain may have only elements of B(L) as metacomponents. The graphical interpretation of a rule-chain is simple: Start at any node and trace a path only in the direction in which the arrows point; a list of the rules associated with the nodes that are passed through is a rule-chain.

A rule-chain $r_1, r_2, \ldots, r_n$ is said to have a *loop* joining r_j and r_k if the metaresult of r_j is a metacomponent of r_k and $k < j+1$. Hence, a single-rule recursive definition is a rule-chain with a loop in it. Graphically, a loop exists if, starting from some node and traversing only in the direction of the arrows, the same node can be reencountered in the graph of the language.

A somewhat different condition from enterability, called *cyclic non-nullity*, is necessary to guarantee that the parsing process will eventually terminate. Cyclic non-nullity requires that if there exist a rule-chain with a loop in it, then there be at least one metacomponent of one of the rules in the loop which cannot be (ancestrally) b_1. Using the symbol " $\nprec$ " for the relationship "is not the ancestor of",

$b_1 \nprec b_i$ unless i $= 1$

$b_1 \nprec n_k$ if and only if for every rule with n_k as a metaresult, there is at least one metacomponent p_j such that $b_1 \nprec p_j$.

Cyclic non-nullity is a restriction on R(L), and not on the sequence in which the elements of R(L) are written in some rule-chain. The restriction is required so that each time a loop in a rule-chain is traversed in parsing an accretion, at least one non-null base object is recognized in the input accretion. Again, traversing a loop in the graph of a language is exactly equivalent to the repeated application of a rule (or sequence of rules) in parsing the input accretion.

The occurrence of elements of **B**(L) in a rule causes (an attempt at) the recognition of those base objects in the input accretion; in the case of a grammatical accretion, the base objects are gradually used up in the parsing process. The restriction of cyclic non-nullity requires that if the same rule (or sequence of rules) is repeated in the parsing process, at least one new character from the input accretion must be used up each time the loop in the graph of the language is traversed. If this were not the case, the process of parsing the input accretion might never terminate.

Finally, it should be pointed out that a rule-chain may contain many loops, and these loops may interlock in an arbitrarily complex way. For the restriction of cyclic non-nullity to be satisfied, each possible loop, considered independently, must be cyclically non-null.

The Basic Parsing Philosophy

The three restrictions of the preceding section (enterability, single-headedness, and cyclic non-nullity) are sufficient to guarantee that a set of rules R(L) can be used to recognize the grammaticalness (in a yes-no sense) of an accretion of elements of **B**(L). They do not, however, guarantee that there is a unique way of deciding that an accretion is grammatical. An accretion may have more than one parsing according to the rules R(L).

As an example of a simple language in which non-unique parsing can occur, consider the set of rules:

$$\begin{array}{lll} \mathbf{H} & \mathbf{B} & \text{hb} \\ \mathbf{B} & \mathbf{C} & \text{bc} \\ \mathbf{H} & \text{bc} & \text{hbc} \\ \text{hb} & \mathbf{C} & \text{hbc} \end{array} \qquad (3.16)$$

(A moment's reflection will identify this as the language of "half baked chickens" or, with appropriate substitutions, "square dance records".) Using this grammar, the accretion **HBC** is clearly grammatical (that is, is named by "hbc", which is the head of the language); on the other hand, there are two distinct parsings:

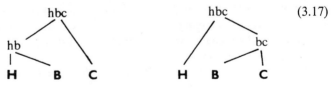

$$(3.17)$$

The simplest parsing philosophy is to start at the top of a list of rules, run down the list until an applicable rule is found, apply it, and repeat the process as often as necessary. This philosophy, when applied to 3.16, would produce the left-hand parsing of 3.17. A rearrangement of the rules, but using the same parsing philosophy, would produce the other parsing of 3.17.

The simple statement of the parsing philosophy leaves much to be desired. In the first place, it is not always obvious that a rule is (or is not) applicable, and a method must be given to answer that question. Second, what happens when there is more than one metacomponent, or when a rule has elements of N(L) as metacomponents?

When the question of applicability of a rule arises, there are two additional pieces of data available to the parsing processor. First, either the first unused base object of the input accretion or the last rule used in the parsing process is known. Second, there is some element of N(L) which may be considered to be the goal of the current parsing effort; initially, this is the head of the language. A rule is applicable if:

i. Its first metacomponent is the same as the first datum   (3.18)
   mentioned above, and
ii. There is a rule-chain with this rule as the left-most rule, such
   that the metaresult of the right-most rule in the rule-chain is
   the second datum mentioned above.

The fact that a rule is applicable according to 3.18 does not necessarily mean that it applies. There may be several rules satisfying the two criteria given above, and the wrong one may be selected initially. If this happens, the parsing processor must try the alternative rules. (It is always possible that the rules ultimately turn out to be inapplicable because the input accretion is ungrammatical!) A simple method of finding the rule-chains will be presented in the next section.

The first datum of the preceding paragraph is the datum in hand for some step in the parsing process, and the second datum is the corresponding goal. Each step in the parsing process has a new datum in hand, and may also have a new goal. Consider a rule-chain consisting of rules which have only a single metacomponent. By the definition of a rule-chain, only the left-most rule has an element of **B**(L) as a metacomponent. When the datum in hand is an element of **B**(L), the parsing process must be at the beginning of this particular rule-chain. On the other hand, when the datum in hand is an element of N(L), the parsing process has progressed along the rule-chain, and all of the rules to the left (see 3.15) of the rule whose (only) metacomponent is the datum in hand have been successfully applied. Furthermore, when the datum in hand is an element of **B**(L), it is the first base object in the input accretion that has not otherwise been used in the parsing; that is, this use (selecting this rule-chain) is the first use by the parsing processor of this base object.

When a rule has more than one metacomponent, all of the meta-components must be recognized in the input accretion before the rule has been successfully applied. When these (non-left) metacomponents are elements of **B**(L), the recognition process is a simple comparison with the first unused base object from the input accretion. When a non-left metacomponent which is an element of N(L) is encountered in a rule, the procedure is somewhat different. The element of N(L) is made the goal for the next step in the parsing process, the first unused base object from the input accretion is made the datum in hand for the next step, and the entire parsing process is started over from this new point.

The parsing process, in summary, can be considered as one which follows a rule-chain in which the link from one rule to the next is from metaresult to left-most metacomponent. Whenever a non-left meta-component is found which is an element of **B**(L), it is compared with the first unused base object in the input accretion. When a non-left meta-component which is an element of N(L) is found in a rule, a new parsing is begun, using the element of N(L) as the goal and the first unused base object from the input accretion as the datum in hand.

The interpretation of this parsing philosophy may be made clearer if the diagramming of the input accretion (as given as an example in Chapter 2) is considered an embodiment of the parsing. Figure 3.20 gives the several steps involved in diagramming the accretion

$$\mathbf{A} = \mathbf{B}/(\mathbf{C} + \mathbf{D}) \tag{3.19}$$

using the parsing philosophy outlined in the preceding paragraphs. The determination of applicability of the rules has been assumed, and the trivial steps of recognizing metacomponents which are elements of **B**(L) and of following rule-chains constructed of rules with single meta-components have been abbreviated.

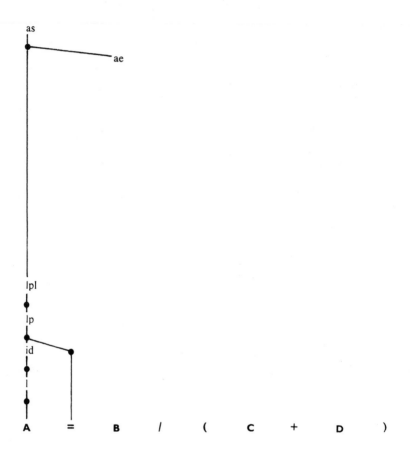

FIG. 3.20.2. A rule-chain of rules with single metacomponents (with the exception of the rule "id = lp", which has only an element of **B**(L) as its second metacomponent) has been found from "**A**" to "as". However, the rule at the head of the rule-chain has a second metacomponent, which is an element of N(L), and a new parsing is required, using "**B**" as the datum in hand and "ae" (the second metacomponent of the rule at the head) as the goal.

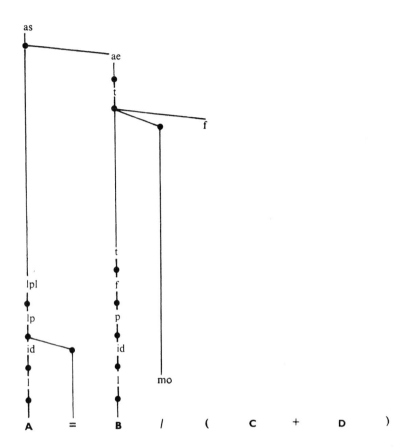

FIG. 3.20.3. A rule-chain from "**B**" to "ae" has been established. The rule at the head of the rule-chain has two additional metacomponents, both of which are elements of N(L), and a rule-chain must be forged between "*/*" and "mo".

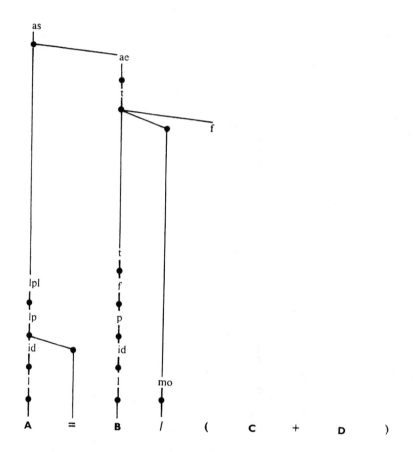

FIG. 3.20.4. The rule-chain desired for the preceding figure consisted of a single rule. A rule-chain must now be forged between "**(**" and "f", which is the third meta-component of the rule at the head of the rule-chain from "**B**" to "ae".

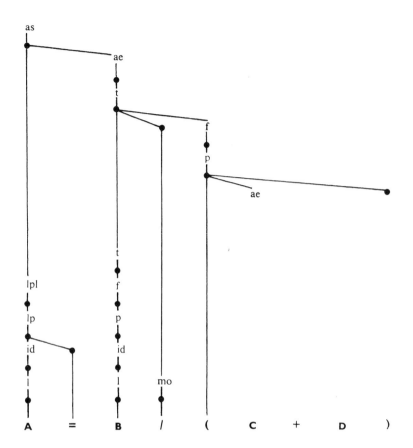

FIG. 3.20.5. There is a rule-chain from "**(**" to "f". However, one of the rules has three metacomponents, and the next metacomponent to be found is an element of N(L). A rule-chain must be forged between "**C**" and "ae". Note the repeated use of rules, equivalent to following a loop around in the graph of the language.

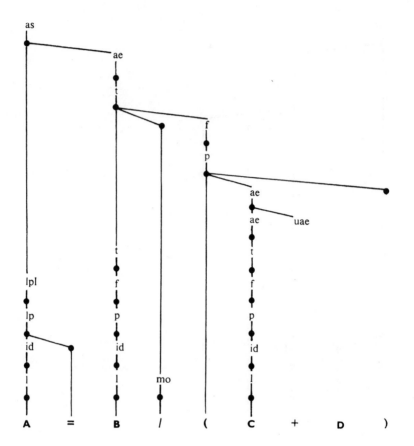

FIG. 3.20.6. The rule-chain from "**C**" to "ae" has been found; however, the rule at its head has a second metacomponent, which is an element of N(L), and a rule-chain is required between it ("uae") and "**+**".

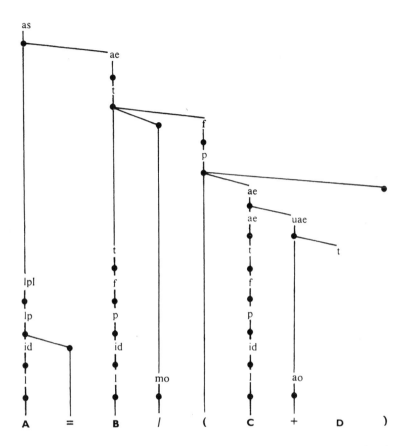

FIG. 3.20.7. The rule-chain from "**+**" to "uae" involves only a single rule, but the rule defining "uae" has a second metacomponent which is an element of N(L).

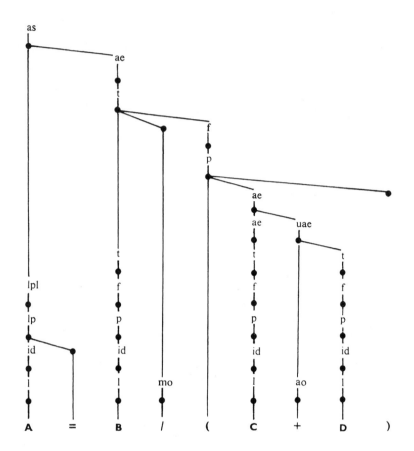

FIG. 3.20.8. A rule-chain for the second metacomponent of the rule defining "uae" has been found, starting with the "**D**" in the input accretion. Since there are no more branches (multiple metacomponents) having precedence, the third meta-component of the rule from 3.20.5 must now be found. It is an element of **B**(L).

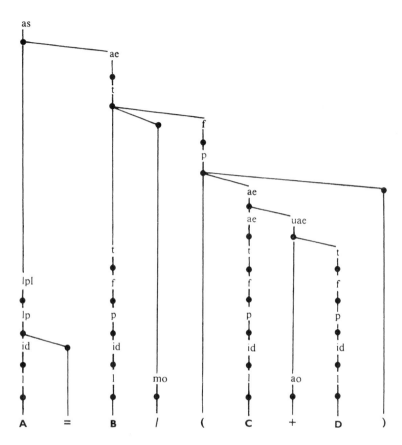

FIG. 3.20.9. The parsing is completed. There are no elements of **B**(L) in the input accretion which have not been used in the parsing, and there are no rules with un-locatable metacomponents. The input accretion is therefore grammatical, according to the rules of 3.9.

The Applicability of a Rule

The question, Is some specific rule applicable?, is equivalent to the question, Is there a rule-chain which leads only through left meta-components from the datum in hand to the goal?. This section is concerned with an algorithm for the production of a table to answer the latter question. This table will have a simple form: Down the side will be a list of possible data that might be in hand, and across will be a list of possible goals. The table entry will be "t" (for "true") when there is a rule-chain from the datum in hand associated with the row to the goal associated with the column, and will be "." otherwise. (Logically, the entry indicating no rule-chain should be "f" for "false"; there are more "f" entries than "t" entries, and the notation selected makes it easier to locate the "t" entries.)

The first step in the algorithm is to form a table of single-rule rule-chains. As the first example set of rules, the simple set from Chapter 2 will be used (in an abbreviated form):

$$
\begin{array}{lllll}
\mathbf{A} & \mathrm{v} & & & \qquad (2.3') \\
\mathbf{B} & \mathrm{v} & & & \\
\mathbf{C} & \mathrm{v} & & & \\
\mathbf{D} & \mathrm{v} & & & \\
\mathbf{E} & \mathrm{v} & & & \\
\mathrm{v} & \mathrm{e} & & & \qquad (2.4') \\
\mathrm{e} & + & \mathrm{v} & \mathrm{e} & \\
\mathrm{v} & = & \mathrm{e} & \mathrm{s} & \qquad (2.5')
\end{array}
$$

The table is formed by labeling the rows with the left metacomponents from the set of rules, starting with elements of N(L). The columns are then labeled in the same manner as the rows, except that no column need be assigned to an element of **B**(L), since elements of **B**(L) cannot occur as metaresults, and hence cannot be goals. Finally, a "t" (for "true") is inserted at the intersection corresponding to the left-metacomponent-row and metaresult-column; this is done for each rule. For the simple grammar, this yields:

$$
\begin{array}{c c c c c}
 & \text{v} & \text{e} & \text{s} & \quad (3.21) \\
\text{v} & . & \text{t} & \text{t} \\
\text{e} & . & \text{t} & . \\
\text{s} & . & . & . \\
\mathbf{A} & \text{t} & . & . \\
\mathbf{B} & \text{t} & . & . \\
\mathbf{C} & \text{t} & . & . \\
\mathbf{D} & \text{t} & . & . \\
\mathbf{E} & \text{t} & . & . \\
\end{array}
$$

If there is a rule-chain from **A** to **B** and a rule-chain from **B** to **C**, then there is a rule-chain from **A** to **C**. A table showing all possible rule-chains is formed from 3.21 by generalizing this statement:

1. Run down the columns starting with the left-hand column; if a "t" is found, do step 2.
2. A "t" has been found in some specific row, say the ith, and in some specific column, say the jth. Find the row which has the same label as the jth column (this will be the jth row). Wherever there is a "t" in this row, put a "t" in the ith row; any "t" already in the ith row remains unchanged. If there are more table entries that have not been scanned by step 1, return to step 1; otherwise, the process is completed.*

If 3.21 is considered a Boolean matrix B[m,n], with m rows and n columns, the algorithm can be expressed quite simply in Algol:

```
for j := 1 step 1 until n do
for i := 1 step 1 until m do
if B[i,j] ∧ i ≠ j then
for k := 1 step 1 until n do
B[i, k] := B[i, k] ∨ B[j, k];
```

The result of applying this algorithm (in either of its two forms!) to 3.21 yields:

---

* A formal equivalence of this algorithm to the extended union of powers of the path matrix is found in [W62].

$$
\begin{array}{c c c c}
 & \text{v} & \text{e} & \text{s} \\
\text{v} & . & \text{t} & \text{t} \\
\text{e} & . & \text{t} & . \\
\text{s} & . & . & . \\
\textbf{A} & \text{t} & \text{t} & \text{t} \\
\textbf{B} & \text{t} & \text{t} & \text{t} \\
\textbf{C} & \text{t} & \text{t} & \text{t} \\
\textbf{D} & \text{t} & \text{t} & \text{t} \\
\textbf{E} & \text{t} & \text{t} & \text{t} \\
\end{array}
\qquad (3.22)
$$

The next step is to add rows to 3.22 for multimetacomponent rules. A row is to be added for each metacomponent (other than the left) which is an element of $N(L)$, and one row is to be added for each such metacomponent in a rule. In the example, there are two such rows to be added; they will be indicated by "p" (for the second rule of 2.4′) and "q" (for 2.5′). The rules for making entries in the added rows are:

   i. A "t" is entered in the column corresponding to the meta-result of the rule containing the metacomponent.

  ii. A "t" is entered in the column corresponding to the meta-result of any rule indistinguishable from the present rule by examination of only the present metacomponent and all metacomponents to its left, providing only that such a rule is physically below the present rule in the sequence in which the rules are presented to the parsing algorithm.

 iii. A "t" is entered wherever there is a "t" in any of the rows corresponding to the metaresults in whose columns a "t" was entered by the first two rules.

This results, from 3.22, in the additional rows:

$$
\begin{array}{c c c c}
 & \text{v} & \text{e} & \text{s} \\
\text{p} & . & \text{t} & . \\
\text{q} & . & . & \text{t} \\
\end{array}
\qquad (3.23)
$$

(The second rule happens to be effectively null in this example.)

The final step in the production of the acceptability table involves the elimination of duplicate rows and columns. If a row has the same entries as some other row, one of the two rows is deleted and the element of $P(L)$ associated with the deleted row is reassociated with the row that was not deleted. In addition, the rows and columns are numbered. This results in:

```
    1 2 3                          (3.24)
1   . t t    v
2   . t .    e,p
3   . . .    s
4   t t t    A,B,C,D,E
5   . . t    q
    v e s
```

One additional observation makes the manual performance of this process simpler. A careful analysis of the process leading from 3.21 to 3.24 will show that duplicate rows (but *not* columns) may be removed at any step in the process by the relabeling technique of the preceding paragraph.*

As a further illustration of the formation of the acceptability table, the procedure described in this section is applied to the rules of Fig. 3.9. Figure 3.25 is analogous to 3.21; it shows single-rule rule-chains. However, duplicate rows have been eliminated, reducing the number of rows from sixty-five to twenty-one. In Fig. 3.26, which is analogous to 3.22, all possible rule-chains have been found, and duplicate rows have again been eliminated. Figure 3.27 is the final acceptability table. The entries resulting from rules with more than one metacomponent are indicated by their rule numbers (enclosed in brackets)† from Fig. 3.9. Duplicate rows have again been eliminated. Figure 3.27 shows the result of eliminating duplicate columns, as well as the assignment of row and column numbers.

At the beginning of this section it was stated that the acceptability table answered the question, Is there a rule-chain which leads only through left metacomponents from the datum in·hand to the desired goal?. In addition, the acceptability table as constructed also answers the question, Can the use of this specific rule, which has more than one metacomponent, possibly lead to the desired goal, given that the left metacomponent is the datum in hand?. Both of these questions may now be referred to the acceptability table for an answer, and the answer is achieved in the same way for both questions. First, the row labeled with

* If duplicate rows are eliminated before the algorithm at the bottom of page 51 is applied, the index "k" must be construed as applying to the original row numbers (that is, the labels of the rows) rather than to the physical position of the rows themselves.

† This method of identifying the metacomponents from the multimetacomponent rules is in general ambiguous, but fails to be in this case because there are no pairs of rules with the same k left metacomponents for other than $k = 1$. Because of this, all of the rows that are added for any given multimetacomponent rule have the same entries.

```
              a a a d d d e f i i l l l m p t u u u
              o e s f n   p   d n   p p o     a i n
                                  l         e
ao            .  .  .  .  .  .  t  .  .  .  .  .  t  .  .
ae, uae       .  t  .  .  .  .  .  .  .  .  .  .  .  .  .
as, in, mo    .  .  .  t  .  .  .  .  .  .  .  .  .  .  .
df            .  .  .  t  .  .  .  .  .  .  .  .  .  .  .
dn, ep        .  .  .  .  .  .  .  .  .  .  .  .  .  .  t
d             .  .  .  .  .  .  .  .  .  .  .  .  .  t  .
f             .  .  .  .  .  t  .  .  .  .  .  t  .  .
id            .  .  .  .  .  .  t  .  .  t  .  t  .
l             .  .  .  .  .  .  t  .  .
lp            .  .  .  .  .  .  .  .  t  .  .  .
lpl           .  .  t  .  .  .  .  .  .  t  .  .  .
p             .  .  .  .  .  t  .  .  .
t             .  t  .  .  .  .  .  .  .  t  .  .  .
ui            .  .  .  t  .  .  .  t  .  .  .  .  t  .
un, (         .  .  .  .  .  .  .  .  .  .  .  t  .
ALL LETTERS   .  .  .  .  .  .  .  .  .  t  .
ALL DIGITS    .  .  .  .  .  t  .  .  .
-, +          t  .  .  .  .  .  .  .  .  .  .  .
*, /          .  .  .  .  .  .  .  .  .  .  t  .
10            .  .  .  .  .  t  .  .  .
.             .  .  .  t  .  .  .  .  .  .
```

FIG. 3.25

```
              a a a d d d e f i i l l l m p t u u u
              o e s f n   p   d n   p p o     a i n
                                  l         e
ao            .  t  .  .  .  .  .  .  t  .  .  .  .  .  t  .  .
ae, uae       .  t  .  .  .  .  .  .  .  .  .  .  .  .  .  .  .
as, in, mo    .  .  .  .  .  .  .  .  .  .  .  .  .  .  .  .  .
df            .  t  .  t  .  t  .  .  .  .  .  t  t  .  .  t
dn, ep        .  t  .  .  .  .  t  .  .  .  .  .  t  t  .  .  t
d, ui         .  t  .  t  .  t  .  t  .  .  .  .  t  t  .  t  t
f, p          .  t  .  .  .  .  t  .  .  .  .  .  .  t  .  .  .
id, l         .  t  t  .  .  .  .  t  t  .  .  t  t  .  t  t  .
lp, lpl       .  .  t  .  .  .  .  .  .  .  .  t  .  .  .  .  .
t             .  t  .  .  .  .  .  .  .  .  .  .  .  t  .  .  .
un, (         .  t  .  .  .  .  t  .  .  .  .  .  t  t  .  .  .
ALL LETTERS   .  t  t  .  .  .  .  t  t  .  t  t  t  .  t  t  .  .  .
ALL DIGITS    .  t  .  .  t  t  .  t  .  t  .  .  .  .  t  t  .  t  t
-, +          t  t  .  .  .  .  .  .  t  .  .  .  .  .  .  t  .  .
*, /          .  .  .  .  .  .  .  .  .  .  .  .  .  t  .  .  .
10            .  t  .  .  .  .  t  t  .  .  .  .  .  .  t  t  .  .  t
.             .  .  t  .  t  t  .  .  t  .  .  .  .  .  t  t  .  .  t
```

FIG. 3.26

the datum in hand (or the rule number, for multimetacomponent rules) is located, as is the column labeled with the goal. If the table entry defined by this process is a "t", then the question is to be answered Yes; otherwise, the question is to be answered No.

	1	2	3	4	5	6	7	8	9	10	11	12	13	14	15	16	17	18	
1	.	t	.	.	.	.	.	.	.	.	t	.	.	.	.	.	t	.	ao
2	.	t	.	.	.	.	.	.	.	.	.	.	.	.	.	.	.	.	ae, uae, [46]
3	.	.	.	.	.	.	.	.	.	.	.	.	.	.	.	.	.	.	as, in, mo
4	.	t	.	.	t	.	.	t	.	.	.	.	.	t	.	.	t	.	df, [67]
5	.	t	.	.	.	.	.	t	.	.	.	.	.	t	.	.	t	.	dn, ep, [48]
6	.	t	.	.	t	.	.	t	.	t	.	.	.	.	t	.	t	t	d, ui, [66]
7	.	t	.	.	.	.	.	t	.	.	.	.	.	.	.	.	.	.	f, p, [52]
8	.	t	t	.	.	.	.	t	t	.	.	t	t	.	t	.	.	.	id, l, [55]
9	.	.	t	.	.	.	.	.	.	.	.	.	t	.	.	.	.	.	lp, lpl, [59]
10	.	t	.	.	.	.	.	.	.	.	.	.	.	.	.	.	.	.	t, [62]
11	.	t	.	.	.	.	.	t	.	.	.	.	.	.	t	.	.	.	un, (, [43]
12	.	t	t	.	.	.	.	t	t	.	t	t	t	.	t	.	.	.	ALL LETTERS
13	.	t	.	.	t	t	.	t	.	t	.	.	.	.	t	.	t	t	ALL DIGITS
14	t	t	.	.	.	.	.	.	.	t	.	.	.	.	.	t	.	.	−, +
15	.	.	.	.	.	.	.	.	.	.	.	t	.	.	.	.	.	.	*, /
16	.	t	.	.	.	t	t	.	.	.	.	.	.	t	.	.	t	.	10, [41]
17	.	t	.	t	t	.	.	t	.	.	.	.	.	t	.	.	t	.	., [42]
18	.	t	.	.	.	.	.	.	.	.	.	.	.	t	.	.	.	.	[44]
19	.	.	.	.	.	.	.	.	t	.	.	.	.	.	.	.	.	.	[45]
20	.	.	t	.	.	.	.	.	.	.	.	.	.	.	.	.	.	.	[60]
	a	a	a	d	d	d	e	f	i	i	l	l	l	m	p	u	u	u	
	o	e	s	f	n		p	&	d	n		p	p	o		a	i	n	
						t						l			e				

F<small>IG</small>. 3.27

The row and column numbers which are assigned to the acceptability table are not particularly useful to persons using the table. They will be used in a later section to form the link between the grammar and the acceptability table.

The Canonical Ordering of P(L)

The notion of a rule as a transition suggests a method for imposing a partial ordering on the elements of P(L). For this purpose, consider that there is a transition between each of the metacomponents of a rule and its metaresult. The set of rules R(L) then generates a list of ordered pairs

(p_i,p_j), where p_i is a metacomponent and p_j is a metaresult. (An ordered pair is generated for each metacomponent of a multimetacomponent rule.) Duplicate pairs, and pairs of the form (p_i,p_i), are excluded from the list. In a given pair, the metacomponent *precedes* the metaresult. The remainder of this section will be devoted to a method for imposing a partial ordering on the elements of P(L) which satisfies the notion of "nearness" to the head of the language L in the sense of Fig. 3.14.

The list of ordered pairs derived from the rules of Fig. 3.9 is given below. As a convenience, and to reduce the number of pairs that must be considered, the pairs **(A**,1), **(B**,1), ..., **(Z**,1) are represented by the single pair $(\lambda,1)$; similarly, the pairs **(0**,d), ..., **(9**,d) are represented by the single pair (δ,d). This has the effect of removing the letters and digits from the domain of the algorithm to be described; the algorithm would not impose an ordering on them in any case, and the usual ordering is acceptable. The list of pairs, then, is:

(t, ae)	(in, ep)	((, p)
(uae, ae)	(↑, f)	(), p)
(+, ao)	(p, f)	(ae, p)
(−, ao)	(l, id)	(id, p)
(ae, as)	(ao, in)	(un, p)
(lpl, as)	(ui, in)	(f, t)
(δ, d)	(λ, l)	(mo, t)
(., df)	(=, lp)	(ao, uae)
(ui, df)	(id, lp)	(t, uae)
(df, dn)	(lp, lpl)	(d, ui)
(ui, dn)	(*, mo)	(ep, un)
(₁₀, ep)	(/, mo)	(dn, un)

If there are any loops in the graph of the language (e.g. Fig. 3.14) which do not result from a single rule, there will be cycles in the list of pairs which will take the form of (p_i,p_j) (p_j,p_k) ... (p_x,p_i). The list of ordered pairs is divided into sublists: The *primary sublist* contains no cycles, and each of the other sublists contains a single cycle. Even in the case of interlocking cycles, it is not necessary to use a pair more than once; the cycles are being eliminated from the original list, and if a pair is moved from the original list into one of the cycle sublists, it cannot contribute to any further cycles in the primary sublist. There are several ways of forming the single cycle sublist from the above table of ordered pairs; one such way yields:

$$(\text{uae, ae}) \ (\text{ae, p}) \ (\text{p, f}) \ (\text{f, t}) \ (\text{t, uae})$$

Start with the head of the language, which must appear in the primary sublist as the metaresult of one or more pairs, and subscript it with the number "0". In the primary sublist, if a metaresult has a subscript k, the metacomponent, if not already subscripted, is subscripted with $(k+1)$. Also, every other appearance of the metacomponent, in all lists and either as metacomponent or metaresult, is also subscripted with $(k+1)$. This process is repeated in the primary sublist until there are no more pairs with both unsubscripted metacomponents and subscripted metaresults.

If an attempt is made to subscript a metaresult in a pair whose metacomponent is already subscripted, and the subscript presently on the metacomponent is not greater than the subscript proposed for the metaresult, all appearances of the metacomponent are desubscripted (including the one in this pair) before the metaresult is subscripted. The normal subscripting process described in the above paragraph then continues.

The normal subscripting process terminates when there are no more pairs in the primary sublist with subscripted metaresults and unsubscripted metacomponents. For the list of pairs given above, this occurs at:

$(+, \text{ao})$	(l_4, id_3)	(un, p)	$(\text{uae}, \text{ae}_1)$
$(-, \text{ao})$	(ao, in)	(mo_3, t_2)	(ae_1, p)
$(\text{ae}_1, \text{as}_0)$	(ui, in)	(ao, uae)	(p, f)
$(\text{lpl}_1, \text{as}_0)$	(λ_5, l_4)	(t_2, ae_1)	(f, t_2)
(δ, d)	$(=_3, \text{lp}_2)$	(d, ui)	(t_2, uae)
$(., \text{df})$	$(\text{id}_3, \text{lp}_2)$	(ep, un)	
(ui, df)	$(\text{lp}_2, \text{lpl}_1)$	(dn, un)	
(df, dn)	$(*_4, \text{mo}_3)$		
(ui, dn)	$(/_4, \text{mo}_3)$		
(l_0, ep)	$((, \text{p})$		
(in, ep)	$(), \text{p})$		
$(\uparrow, \text{f})$	(id_3, p)		

After the subscripting of the primary sublist has terminated, the cycle sublists are inspected. The cycle sublist containing the metacomponent with the numerically smallest subscript is located. (There may be more than one such sublist, but the requirement of enterability guarantees at least one.) The pair (or pairs) containing this metacomponent is deleted from the cycle sublist, and the remaining elements of the cycle sublist are added to the primary sublist. The normal subscripting process is then resumed. If more than one metacomponent in a cycle has this same lowest subscript, all such pairs containing all such metacomponents are deleted from the cycle sublist before the remaining pairs are added to the primary sublist. Eventually all of the modified cycle sublists will be included in the primary sublist by this process, and all of the pairs will have both metacomponent and metaresult subscripted.

The list of pairs from the example above that results when the subscripting process is completed is:

$$
\begin{array}{llll}
(+_{10}, ao_9) & (df_8, dn_7) & (\lambda_8, l_7) & (un_6, p_5) \\
(-_{10}, ao_9) & (ui_9, dn_7) & (=_3, lp_2) & (f_4, t_3) \\
(t_3, ae_1) & (_{10_a}, ep_7) & (id_6, lp_2) & (mo_4, t_3) \\
(uae_2, ae_1) & (in_8, ep_7) & (lp_2, lpl_1) & (ao_9, uae_2) \\
(ae_1, as_0) & (\uparrow_5, f_4) & (*_5, mo_4) & (t_3, uae_2) \\
(lpl_1, as_0) & (p_5, f_4) & (/_5, mo_4) & (d_{10}, ui_9) \\
(\delta_{11}, d_{10}) & (l_7, id_6) & ((_6, p_5) & (ep_7, un_6) \\
(._a, df_8) & (ao_9, in_8) & ()_6, p_5) & (dn_7, un_6) \\
(ui_9, df_8) & (ui_9, in_8) & (id_6, p_5) &
\end{array}
$$

Finally, from this list of pairs, a table is formed:

subscript	B(L)	N(L)
0		as
1		ae lpl
2		uae lp
3	=	t
4		f mo
5	↑ * /	p
6	( )	id un
7		dn ep l
8	$_{10}\lambda$	df in
9	.	ao ui
10	+ −	d
11	δ	

A partial ordering can finally be imposed on P(L) by reading up the **B**(L) column and then up the N(L) column of this table. No ordering is established between elements of **B**(L) or of N(L) which have the same subscript. Hence, *one* of the canonical orderings for the elements of P(L) is:

$$P(L) = \{0,1,2,3,4,5,6,7,8,9,+,-,.,_{10},A,B,C,D,E,F,G,H,I,J,K,$$
$$L,M,N,O,P,Q,R,S,T,U,V,W,X,Y,Z,(,),\uparrow,*,/,=,$$
$$d,ao,ui,df,in,dn,ep,l,id,un,p,f,mo,t,uae,lp,ae,lpl,as\}$$

The other canonical orderings result from permutations of the elements of **B**(L) and N(L) which have the same subscripts in the table.

The Parsing Form of a Grammar

Figure 3.9 was an example of a grammar. Several minor changes in form may be made to such a grammar which will facilitate the parsing of an input accretion by either a human or a computer.

Before a grammar can be used efficiently by a parsing processor, it is desirable that rules which represent alternative choices at each stage of the parsing be grouped together in the grammar; this reduces the amount of time necessary for searching the grammar for the applicable rule. Such an *acceptable arrangement of the grammar* is one which satisfies the two criteria:

i. For every pair of rules and for all values of k: If two rules have the same first k constituents (counting from left to right and including both metacomponents and metaresults), then any rules which fall between these two rules must also have the same first k constituents.

ii. For all values of k greater than 1: If the first difference between two rules (counting as above) is at the kth constituent, then any significant relative ordering of the two rules can be decided by making metacomponents precede metaresults and elements of **B**(L) as metacomponents precede elements of N(L) as metacomponents.

With the parsing philosophy described earlier in this chapter, the first criterion cannot require a reordering of the rules that would affect the resolution of any question of ambiguity. (The proof of this is left to the reader; it is not difficult.) The second criterion may well require a reordering (to produce an acceptable arrangement) which will result in a different resolution of any ambiguity than that of the original ordering.

There is one particular class of acceptable orderings which may be considered to be canonical. Make the three assumptions that:

i. The constituents of a rule are considered to be written in columns in a positional notation, with the left-most constituent in the most significant column and blanks filled in as needed on the right;

ii. The canonical order for the possible constituents is that of the ordered set $P(L)$; and

iii. A blank in a column is of more significance than any element of $P(L)$ in that column.

Under these assumptions, the normal sorting procedure applied to the elements of $R(L)$ will result in one of the canonical acceptable arrangements. The number of canonical acceptable arrangements is usually greater than one because $P(L)$ is in general only partially ordered.

The result of placing the grammar of Chapter 2 (which has been used earlier in this chapter as an example) into an acceptable arrangement gives

$$
\begin{array}{llll}
\mathbf{A} & v & & \\
\mathbf{B} & v & & \\
\mathbf{C} & v & & \\
\mathbf{D} & v & & \\
\mathbf{E} & v & & \\
v & = & e & s \\
v & e & & \\
e & + & v & e
\end{array}
\qquad (3.28)
$$

A second addition to the form of $R(L)$ makes references to the acceptability table easier for either human or compiler. A reference to the acceptability table involves a search of both of the row labels (for the datum in hand) and the column labels (for the goal). The searching can be eliminated if references to the explicit row or column are associated with the constituents of the rules. The row and column numbers associated with the constituents are determined by four rules:

i. A left metacomponent which is an element of **B**(L) has associated with it the row number of the row it labels.

ii. A left metacomponent which is an element of N(L) has associated with it first the row number of the row it labels and second the column number of the column it labels.

iii. A non-left metacomponent of a multimetacomponent rule which is an element of N(L) has associated with it the row number of the row labeled with the rule number of the rule in which it appears.

iv. A metaresult has associated with it the row number of the row which it labels.

A non-left metacomponent which is an element of **B**(L) has neither row nor column number associated with it.

Finally, a *pseudo-rule* is placed at the end of the grammar for each element of N(L) that does not occur as a left metacomponent. With each such pseudo-rule is associated the column number of the column which it labels. Using 3.28 as a grammar and 3.24 as an acceptability table, this yields

$$
\begin{array}{lll}
\textbf{A},4 & \text{v},1 & \\
\textbf{B},4 & \text{v},1 & \\
\textbf{C},4 & \text{v},1 & \\
\textbf{D},4 & \text{v},1 & \\
\textbf{E},4 & \text{v},1 & \\
\text{v},1,1 & = & \text{e},5 \quad \text{s},3 \\
\text{v},1,1 & \text{e},2 & \\
\text{e},2,2 & + & \text{v},2 \quad \text{e},2 \\
\text{s},3 & &
\end{array}
$$

As a final example of the results of this section, the set of rules from Fig. 3.9 (which are already in an acceptable, but not a canonical, arrangement) are shown in Fig. 3.29 with links to the acceptability table of Fig. 3.27. The rule numbers (in brackets) follow the rules, as they did in Fig. 3.9. Care must be taken to distinguish between the lower-case "l" and the number "1".

A,12	l,8	[1]
B,12	l,8	[2]
C,12	l,8	[3]
D,12	l,8	[4]
E,12	l,8	[5]
F,12	l,8	[6]
G,12	l,8	[7]
H,12	l,8	[8]
I,12	l,8	[9]
J,12	l,8	[10]
K,12	l,8	[11]
L,12	l,8	[12]
M,12	l,8	[13]
N,12	l,8	[14]
O,12	l,8	[15]
P,12	l,8	[16]
Q,12	l,8	[17]
R,12	l,8	[18]
S,12	l,8	[19]
T,12	l,8	[20]
U,12	l,8	[21]
V,12	l,8	[22]
W,12	l,8	[23]
X,12	l,8	[24]
Y,12	l,8	[25]
Z,12	l,8	[26]
0,13	d,6	[27]
1,13	d,6	[28]
2,13	d,6	[29]
3,13	d,6	[30]
4,13	d,6	[31]
5,13	d,6	[32]
6,13	d,6	[33]
7,13	d,6	[34]
8,13	d,6	[35]
9,13	d,6	[36]

−,14	ao,1	[37]		
+,14	ao,1	[38]		
*,15	mo,3	[39]		
/,15	mo,3	[40]		
$_{10}$,16	in,16	ep,5	[41]	
.,17	ui,17	df,4	[42]	
(,11	ae,11	)	p,7	[43]
ao,1,1	t,18	uae,2	[44]	
ao,1,1	ui,19	in,3	[45]	
ae,2,2	uae,2	ae,2	[46]	
df,4,4	dn,5	[47]		
dn,5,5	ep,5	un,11	[48]	
dn,5,5	un,11	[49]		
d,6,6	ui,6	[50]		
ep,5,7	un,11	[51]		
f,7,8	↑	p,7	f,7	[52]
f,7,8	t,10	[53]		
id,8,9	=	lp,9	[54]	
id,8,9	l,8	id,8	[55]	
id,8,9	p,7	[56]		
l,8,11	id,8	[57]		
lp,9,12	lpl,9	[58]		
lpl,9,13	lp,9	lpl,9	[59]	
lpl,9,13	ae,20	as,3	[60]	
p,7,15	f,7	[61]		
t,10,8	mo,10	f,10	t,10	[62]
t,10,8	ae,2	[63]		
uae,2,16	ae,2	[64]		
un,11,18	p,7	[65]		
ui,6,17	d,6	ui,6	[66]	
ui,6,17	df,4	dn,5	[67]	
ui,6,17	dn,5	[68]		
ui,6,17	in,3	[69]		
as,3				
in,10				
mo,14				

FIG. 3.29

CHAPTER 4

Details of a Parsing Processor

A typical parsing processor is comprised of four basic sections: *initialization, processing, recovery*, and *output*; their interrelationship is shown diagrammatically in Fig. 4.1 (and in greater detail in Figs. 4.9, 4.10, 4.11, and 4.12). The initialization section sets up goals and subgoals for the other sections; initially, the goal is the head of the language, but subgoals are required whenever a rule has a non-left metacomponent that is an element of N(L). The processing section builds the parsing tree from the base objects of the input accretion toward the current goal. If it encounters a non-left metacomponent which is an element of N(L), it reenters the initialization section to establish a subgoal; if a particular rule does not apply, the recovery section is entered in an attempt to find an alternative rule; and finally, the output section is entered when the current goal has been unambiguously achieved.

The recovery section is entered when a change must be made in some facet of the current processing; the most frequent case is that the rule currently being used by the processing section turns out not to be in a rule-chain toward the current goal. Alternatively, entrance is made when the output section has completed its writing and some previous level of the parsing (which was interrupted to identify some subgoal) may be resumed. The exit that is made from the recovery section indicates the way in which recovery was made; this will be discussed in detail below.

The output section produces the output of the parsing process in a modified suffix form. Output is produced whenever the processing section has found a rule-chain between the input accretion and the current goal.

Sufficient records of the output are kept so that spurious outputs (which may result if part of an accretion is grammatical but some later part is not) will be overwritten.

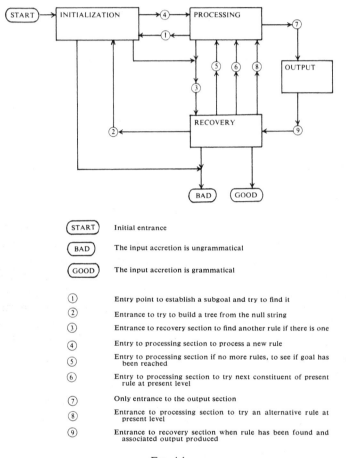

FIG. 4.1

The remainder of this chapter will discuss the particular form of the output that is generated by the parsing processor, as well as the details of the parsing processor itself.

The Output of the Parsing Processor

The output of the parsing processor is the parsing tree, as illustrated in Fig. 3.20.9. The form illustrated, however, is not convenient for a computer to generate, and is even more difficult for a computer to reprocess. A preferable notation, therefore, is one which reduces a tree to a linear accretion.

The easiest way of describing the particular representation of a tree that is the output of the parsing processor is by an example. Consider the tree

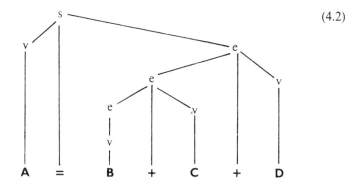

(4.2)

which represents the parsing of the accretion "**A = B + C + D**" with the rules of 3.28. The *suffix form of a tree* is generated from a tree by tracing out a path which always goes to the right and down, and returns to the right-most lowest, untraversed branch when there is nowhere else to go. A node is written into the suffix form when it is traversed by such a path. The result of thus traversing 4.2 (the suffix form of the tree 4.2) is:

$$s \; e \; v \; \mathbf{D} + e \; v \; \mathbf{C} + e \; v \; \mathbf{B} = v \; \mathbf{A} \qquad (4.3)$$

The form of 4.3 can be shortened by remembering that the use of a rule implies the successful recognition of all of the metacomponents of the rule. As a consequence, if it is known which rule has been applied, there is no necessity to indicate the elements of B(L) which appear as metacomponents. One method of indicating the particular rule that was used is to number the rules in R(L) and to use the rule number rather than the metaresult. The rules, with the rule numbers indicated in brackets, are:

$$
\begin{array}{llllll}
\textbf{A} & v & [1] & & & \\
\textbf{B} & v & [2] & & & \\
\textbf{C} & v & [3] & & & \\
\textbf{D} & v & [4] & & & \\
\textbf{E} & v & [5] & & & \\
v & = & e & s & [6] & \\
v & e & [7] & & & \\
e & + & v & e & [8] &
\end{array}
\qquad (3.28')
$$

and the result of rewriting 4.3 is simply:

$$
6\ 8\ 4\ 8\ 3\ 7\ 2\ 1 \qquad (4.4)
$$

The use of the output of the parsing processor as an input to the unparsing processor imposes an additional restriction of convenience on the output: Each entry in the output which represents a metaresult must be followed by exactly as many entries as there are metacomponents of that rule which are elements of N(L). It is obvious that this condition is not met by 4.3, less so by 4.4, and cannot be met in general by the suffix form of a tree as described above. This restriction requires that a new form of entry—a *link*—be introduced in the output of the parsing processor. A link may be considered as a pointer to a list of entries which, were it not for the restriction stated above, would have been written instead of the link.

The introduction of links is best illustrated from 4.3. Starting at the left-hand end of the suffix form of the tree, locate the first entry which represents a non-leftmost metacomponent of a multimetacomponent rule. This entry is the head of a subtree of the parsing tree (or is an element of **B**(L)). The entries representing this subtree are moved to the left of the parsing tree representation, and a link is inserted which points to the new location.

The entire tree is again scanned from left to right, and additional links inserted according to the same rule. The steps involved in introducing links into 4.3 are:

s e v **D +** e v **C +** e v **B** = v **A**   (4.3)

e v **D +** e v **C** + e v **B** s   = v **A**

v **D** e   + e v **C +** e v **B** s   = v **A**

+ v **D** e   e v **C +** e v **B** s   = v **A**

v **C +** v **D** e   e   + e v **B** s   = v **A**

+ v **C +** v **D** e   e   e v **B** s   = v **A**   (4.5)

(The " **=** " should also move, according to the rules, but it is unimportant.)

The analogous operations may be performed on the rule-number representation of 4.4 to give:

6 8 4 8 3 7 2 1   (4.4)

8 4 8 3 7 2 6   1

4 8   8 3 7 2 6   1

3 4 8   8   7 2 6   1   (4.6)

The reduction in the number of links necessary in 4.6, as compared with 4.5, is a consequence of the use of rule numbers and the fact that the elements of B(L) appearing as metacomponents may be implied, rather than stated explicitly.

The representation, with the included links, seems on first sight to be trading one two-dimensional representation for another. This is easily resolved; one method, and the one used in the parsing processor, is the equivalent of numbering the entries from left to right and replacing the link with the entry number to which it points. In order to distinguish links from rule numbers, an artifice must be introduced such as indicating the links as negative numbers. For 4.6, this gives:

3 4 8 −2 8 −1 7 2 6 −3 1   (4.7)

One final link is added at the right, pointing to the head of the tree. This link is the only way the unparsing processor can identify the head of the parsing tree, since the head is no longer at an end of the representation.

$$3\ 4\ 8\ -2\ 8\ -1\ 7\ 2\ 6\ -3\ 1\ -9 \tag{4.8}$$

A Detailed Flow-Chart of the Parsing Processor

Figures 4.9 through 4.12 are detailed flow-charts of the four parts of the parsing processor shown in diagrammatic form in Fig. 4.1. These four flow-charts are designed for people, rather than for coding on a machine, and therefore describe the parsing process, rather than dissect it.

Three operations are used in these flow-charts which are operations on *lists,* rather than on single values. Such a list has two parts: the *head,* which is directly accessible to a processor, and the *tail,* which is not. Any reference to the *value of a list* is to the current value of the head of the list (and if the head of the list does not have a value, then neither does the list). The value of the head of a list may be *preserved* by being copied into the tail of the list, while leaving the value of the head unchanged. A list may be *restored* by moving the most recently preserved value from the tail of the list to its head; this operation removes the entry from the tail of the list and destroys whatever the previous value of the head may have been. Finally, a value may be *lost* from a list: the most recently preserved value is removed from the tail of the list and thrown away, leaving the head unchanged. As an example of the meaning of these list operations, a sequence of commands is shown below, together with the list being manipulated. The head of the list is to the left of the "|", and the tail to the right:

1 into *LIST*	1|
preserve *LIST*	1|1
LIST+2 into *LIST*	3|1
preserve *LIST*	3|3 1
5 into *LIST*	5|3 1
lose *LIST*	5|1
restore *LIST*	1|

The tail of a list behaves like a last-in-first-out list [N60a].

There are nine lists used in Figs. 4.9 through 4.12. Four of them are associated with the current goal of the parsing process, and another four are associated with the datum in hand. The final list is used in converting the parsing tree to the modified suffix form described in the preceding section.

The Initialization Section

The initialization section of the parsing processor is invoked whenever a new goal must be established as a consequence of a rule's being used which has an element of N(L) as other than a left-most metacomponent. Figure 3.20, which was an illustration of the parsing of an assignment statement, can also be used to show the functions of the various parts of the parsing process. Each place in Fig. 3.20 where a new goal is established appears as a branch coming down and to the right from the already-established tree; these branches are established by the initialization section by making the nodes at their ends into subgoals for further parsing.

The establishment of a subgoal is done by preserving and then assigning new values to the four lists *GOAL, INPUT, OUTPUT,* and *NULL*:

GOAL has as its value the current goal;

INPUT has as its value a pointer to the base object of the input accretion at which parsing started for the current goal;

OUTPUT has as its value a pointer to the output cell at which the first output produced by the scanning for the current goal will be written; and

NULL has the value "0" if the parsing for the current goal started with a base object from the input accretion, and a value "1" if the scanning began from an assumed $\mathbf{b}_1$ between *INPUT* and $(INPUT-1)$.

As the list *GOAL* is defined, its value is an element of N(L) rather than a number. This makes a description of the parsing process simpler, and any particular implementation can map from the elements of N(L) into the integers as an internal representation [I62].

There are three entrances to and three exits from the initialization section of the parsing process. The initial entry (labeled "START") is made only once; if there is no rule-chain from either $\mathbf{b}_1$ or from the first base object of the input accretion to the head of the language, the input accretion is *prima facie* ungrammatical, and exit is made at once to "BAD". Normally, the input accretion is at least potentially gram-

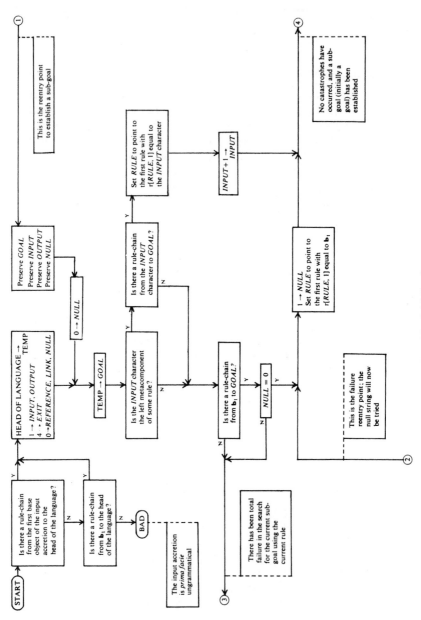

FIG. 4.9. Initialization.

matical, and the exit is made through the connector* numbered "4";
this path through the initialization section sets the values of the four lists
described in the preceding paragraph.

The entrance through the connector numbered "1" is the normal
reentry point. This reentry is made whenever the processing section (to
be described next) needs to have a new subgoal established; this happens
for each non-first metacomponent of a rule which is also an element of
N(L). Entrance 1 causes the four lists (*GOAL, INPUT, OUTPUT,
NULL*) to be preserved and new values to be given to the heads of the
lists to establish the required element of N(L) as a new goal.

Entry is made through the connector numbered "2" when there has
been no success in the parsing; if b_1 has not been used as a possible
character to initiate parsing for the current goal, it will be tried, and
exit will be made through connector "4". If, on the other hand, b_1 has
already been tried, then the condition of cyclic non-nullity (see Chapter 3)
requires that a failure be assumed; in this case, exit is made to the
recovery section through connector "3".

The Processing Section

The processing section attempts to build a rule-chain from the left-
most unused base character of the input accretion to the current goal, as
established by the most recent entry to the initialization section.

The processing section maintains four lists:

EXIT, whose value determines the path to be taken out of the processing section when a parsing has been completed or when it
has been determined that a parsing is impossible;

RULE, whose value is the rule number of the rule currently being
used in the parsing process;

CONSTITUENT, whose value is a pointer to the particular constituent of the rule whose number is the value of *RULE* and which
is currently being processed; and

REFERENCE, whose value is an indication of the number of metacomponents of the current rule which are elements of N(L) and
have been processed.

The values of *RULE* and *CONSTITUENT* are conveniently consid-
ered as being row and column in the matrix which was postulated in
Chapter 3 for the generation of the canonical ordering of the rules.
This matrix is denoted "r" in the flow-charts. The value of *REFER-
ENCE* is used to determine the number of links that must be written

---

* A connector on the flow charts is symbolized by a circled number.

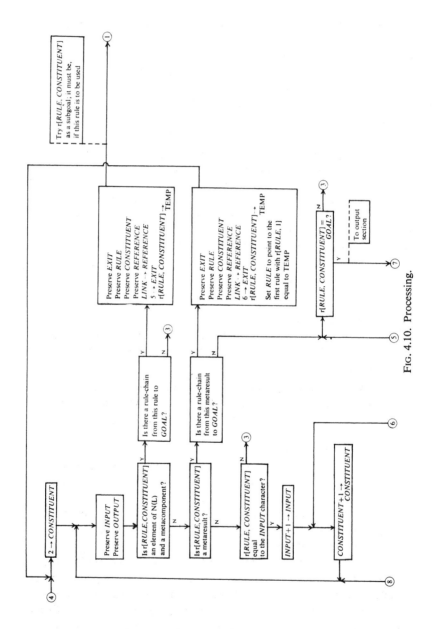

FIG. 4.10. Processing.

in the output for a particular subtree; links, in this sense, were described earlier, in the section on the output form of the parsing processor. The particular way in which the number of links is indicated is discussed with the output section of the parsing processor.

The processing section has four entrances (connectors 4, 5, 6, and 8) and three exits (connectors 1, 3, and 7). The normal entrance is connector 4, and the normal exit is connector 7.

Entrance at connector 4 starts to build branches of the parsing tree up from the first unused base object of the input accretion towards the current goal (as established by the most recent invocation of the initialization section).

Entrance at connector 5 is made from the recovery section when there are no more applicable rules. This may indicate either that the input accretion is ungrammatical with respect to the particular rules that have been attempted (resulting in another attempt being made at a higher level) or that the desired element of $N(L)$ has been found; in the former case, exit is made back to the recovery section through connector 3, and in the latter, exit is made to the output section through connector 8.

Entrance is made at connector 6 from the recovery section when a subtree has been found which defines the element of $N(L)$ (used as a non-first metacomponent) which initiated the search for the subtree by reentering the initialization section.

Finally, entrance is made at connector 8 when a particular rule has proven not to be applicable (in some particular instance) and an alternative rule is to be tried.

Whenever entrance is made through connectors 1, 6, and 8, the lists *INPUT* and *OUTPUT* are preserved in case it is later necessary to back up.

Exit through connector 1 is made when a new subgoal must be established by the initialization section. Exit is made through connector 3 to the recovery section and through connector 7 to the output section.

The Recovery Section

The initialization and processing sections use their lists to keep track of the place in the rules, the input accretion, and the output. Preservation of these lists, and the changing of their values, is done in the initialization and processing sections; the lists are restored, however, in the recovery sections, where it is also determined what further action should be taken (i.e. what section should be invoked after exit is made from the recovery section).

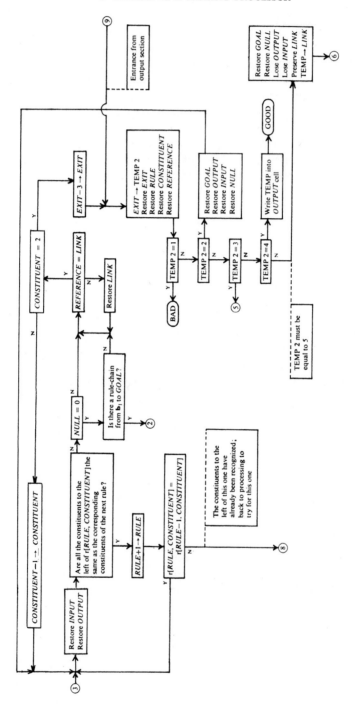

FIG. 4.11. Recovery.

The two entrances to the recovery section are connectors 3 and 9. Connector 3 is the normal entry point, connector 9 being only the return from the output section. The exits from the recovery section are connectors 2, 5, 6, 8 and the two main exits from the entire parsing processor, GOOD and BAD.

Entry is made to the recovery section when another section has reached a point where there is nothing more that it can do.

Exit is made through connector 2 when an attempt to locate a subtree of the parsing tree whose head is some element of N(L) has failed completely. The element of N(L) was a non-left metacomponent of some rule; an attempt will be made to find an alternative rule, not using this particular metacomponent, at the same level.

Exit is made through connector 5 when no other branches can be added to the subtree that has been developed at the current level of parsing, but there is a possibility that the head of the subtree may be the subgoal that is desired, rather than merely a step towards it.

Exit is made through connector 6 when an attempt to locate a subtree of the parsing tree whose head is some element of N(L) has been successful. The element of N(L) was a non-left metacomponent of some rule and the result of its having been found is to allow the rule to continue to be used in the parsing.

Exit is made through connector 8 when there are alternative rules available at the current level of parsing, but the particular rule being tried has failed. Because of the requirement (see Chapter 3) that the rules be in an acceptable arrangement, alternative rules (defined operationally as those which differ from each other, scanning from the left, at the component whose value is the value of the list *CONSTITUENT*) will follow each other in the table of rules.

Exit through the main exits from the parsing processor, GOOD and BAD, indicate successful or unsuccessful parsing of the input accretion, respectively.

The Output Section

The output section of the parsing processor is invoked whenever a rule-chain has been completed from a base character in the input accretion to the current subgoal of the parsing processor.

Since the value of *OUTPUT* is the pointer to the cell in the output in which the first part of the output will be written, its negative is stored to serve as a link for the tree of which the current output constitutes a sub-tree; see above, in this chapter, where the form of the output of the parsing processor is discussed at length.

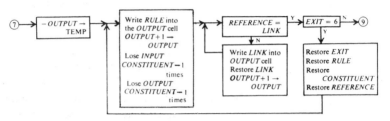

FIG. 4.12. Output.

Next, the main writing loop is entered. A rule number is written out followed by zero or more links, as determined by comparing the values of *LINK* and *REFERENCE*. The value of *REFERENCE* was set to the value that *LINK* had at the beginning of the processing for the corresponding rule. Hence, if *LINK* and *REFERENCE* are the same at the end of the processing, no links need be written out, while if there is a difference, the entries from *LINK* are written until the one corresponding to the value of *REFERENCE* is restored. Also, since it is clear at this point that a rule has been used successfully, those values of *INPUT* and *OUTPUT* that were preserved in case of backup are lost.

Exit is made from the output section when a rule is encountered (in the process of restoring the various lists) whose processing is not yet complete. (The processing of a rule is complete when every metacomponent which is an element of N(L) has been processed as a subgoal of the parsing processor; that is, when all of the subtrees pendent from the rule have been constructed.)

CHAPTER 5

Some Extensions to the Metasyntactic Language

There are a number of features in the languages that are currently being developed which require more mechanism than the metasyntactic language of Chapter 3 and the parsing processor of Chapter 4 can provide.* The particular additional features vary from language to language, and all that can be done in this chapter is to indicate a number of extensions that have been found to be useful, the way of including them in the parsing processor of Chapter 4, and the general technique by which additional extensions may be made when the need arises. These extensions will be referred to as *metasyntactic functions* (MSFs).

The general notation that will be used for an MSF is to indicate the particular type of function between the special brackets "«" and "»". An MSF is considered a unary operator; depending on the specific type of MSF, it may be either prefixed or suffixed to the metacomponent which is its operand. However, the MSF is usually a function on the endpoints of the subtree whose head is the operand of the MSF, rather than a function on the operand itself. Assuming prefixed MSFs, in the rule

$$a \quad «1» \quad b \quad c \quad «2» \quad d \quad e \tag{5.1}$$

the MSF "«1»" operates on the metacomponent "b", and the MSF "«2»" operates on the metacomponent "d".

In 5.1, the metacomponent "b" is an element of N(L). Suppose that

---

* This statement is likely to be true at any point in time.

the rule by which it was recognized (that is, the rule in which "b" appears as a metaresult) also contained a (prefixed) MSF:

$$p \quad \text{«3»} \quad q \quad b$$

In the process of recognizing the metacomponents "p" and "q", it must be remembered that the endpoints of the subtrees which they head are within the scope of the MSF "«1»", while the endpoints of the subtree headed by "q" are also within the scope of the "«3»".

In the case where more than one MSF operates on a given meta-component, the priority of interpretation of the MSFs is:

(a) Prefixed MSFs are functional during the process of recognition; the innermost MSF operates first, then the next innermost, and so on.

(b) Suffixed MSFs are functional only after the recognition of the metacomponent has been completed; again, the innermost MSF functions first, then the next innermost, and so on.

The Substitution MSF

It is often useful, in the process of parsing an input accretion, to be able to ignore certain base objects and to be able to make substitutions for other base objects. In translating mechanical languages such as Fortran or Algol, these substitutions are most frequently necessary for blanks and punctuation marks [H64]. In natural languages the substitutions are more involved; as an example, it may be desirable to substitute, for an irregular form of a verb, a regularized form indicating explicitly the implicit information of the irregular form.

The general problem is to substitute any object (accretion of base objects, a single base object, or the null object*) for any instance of a member of a subset of the set $\mathbf{B}(L)$. This is conveniently symbolized by a prefixed

$$\text{«}\alpha \rightarrow \{\mathbf{b}_{s_1}, \mathbf{b}_{s_2}, \ldots, \mathbf{b}_{s_i}\}\text{»} \tag{5.2}$$

---

* The null object is quite different from the null string. In the context of scanning an accretion, the null object may be thought of as something which is simply ignored in the scanning process (i.e. never delivered for further processing), while the null string may be thought of as an indication that something which might have been syntactically permissible was not in the input accretion, and that its absence is also (locally) syntactically permissible.

in which α denotes the object being substituted, and the subset of elements of $\mathbf{B}(L)$ are those base objects for which the substitution is to be made. If it is intended to substitute the null object, 5.2 becomes simply

$$«\rightarrow\{\mathbf{b}_{s_1}, \ldots\}»$$ (5.3)

In the case where the subset of $\mathbf{B}(L)$ consists of a single element, it may be written without the surrounding "{" and "}". Finally, it is explicitly permitted that a substitution be made for $\mathbf{b}_1$.

The substitution of the null object for an element of $\mathbf{B}(L)$ has the effect of treating the element of $\mathbf{B}(L)$ as though it had simply vanished from the input accretion; in other words, as though that element of $\mathbf{B}(L)$ was not to be considered *in any way* by the parsing processor.

A substitution for the base object $\mathbf{b}_1$ is effective only at those points in the input accretion where the parsing processor looks for $\mathbf{b}_1$ (see Fig. 4.9), rather than between each of the base objects of the input accretion. The substitution takes place after the $\mathbf{b}_1$ is recognized, but before it is processed. This case is somewhat different from substitutions for other elements of $\mathbf{B}(L)$, which can take place external to the parsing processor (albeit dynamically, since a given portion of the input accretion may be scanned several times, each time under the scope of a different MSF).

The effect of the MSF

$$«\rightarrow\mathbf{b}_1»$$ (5.4)

is therefore to suppress the processing of $\mathbf{b}_1$ in the same general way that the substitution of the null object for any element of $\mathbf{B}(L)$ prevents its being processed by the parsing processor. (The details, however, differ: For all elements of $\mathbf{B}(L)$ except $\mathbf{b}_1$, the deletion is accomplished at the point where the parsing processor requests another element of $\mathbf{B}(L)$ from the input accretion; for $\mathbf{b}_1$, the recognition takes place inside the parsing processor itself, and therefore so must the elimination.)

The examples of the introductory paragraph may be symbolized to provide further illustration. A substitution MSF which will, informally, cause spaces to be ignored from the input accretion, may be given by

$$«\rightarrow\sqcup»$$

As a more complicated example, drawn from natural languages, it may be desirable, in the scanning of an input accretion, to replace the irregular form of the verb "to be", "was", with the infinitive and an indication of tense, number, and person:

«be + past + singular + 1st or 3rd person → was»

The implementation of the substitution MSF in the sense of the parsing processor of Chapter 4 requires two basic changes. First, an additional list, *SUBSTITUTION*, is required, into which the substitution MSFs can be stored. This list is manipulated as follows:

(a) Whenever the list *GOAL* is preserved, the value of *SUBSTITUTION* is made equal to the value of *GOAL*, and then *SUBSTITUTION* is preserved.

(b) Whenever *GOAL* is lost or restored, *SUBSTITUTION* is restored until its value is a goal rather than an MSF.

(c) Whenever a substitution MSF is encountered as a metacomponent, it is placed in the head of *SUBSTITUTION*, and the list is then preserved.

(d) Whenever an element of **B**(L) is encountered as a non-left metacomponent, step (b) must be executed to restore *SUBSTITUTION*, since a recursion did not take place as a part of the recognition of the element of **B**(L).

The list *SUBSTITUTION* is slightly different from the other lists in the parsing processor. Like the other lists, its head may be inspected at any time; unlike them, its tail may also be inspected.

The second change that must be made in the parsing processor to implement the substitution MSF requires the scanning of the list *SUBSTITUTION* each time a base object is delivered to the parsing processor, to see whether there are any substitution MSFs applying to it. The list is scanned from newest entry to oldest so that the proper application of the MSFs as unary operators will be preserved. This scanning is done at each point in the parsing processor where a base object is requested from the input accretion; in addition, when the parsing processor has determined that **b**$_1$ should be tried (Fig. 4.9, just prior to the box "1→*NULL*"), *SUBSTITUTION* is also scanned for substitutions for **b**$_1$.

If the null object is substituted for an element of **B**(L) other than **b**$_1$, the effect is as though the base object in the input accretion had been skipped over (or was never there to begin with). If the substitution is for **b**$_1$, exit is made from the initialization section (Fig. 4.9) to the recovery section (Fig. 4.11) via connector 3.

If a single base object is substituted for another, it is simply delivered to the parsing processor in lieu of the object that had been located in the input accretion. In case the substitution was for b_1, the value of *RULE* is set to point to the first rule with $r[RULE,1]$ equal to the base object substituted for b_1, rather than to the first rule with $r[RULE,1]$ equal to b_1.

If an object not a base object is substituted for a base object, the substituted accretion of base objects is treated exactly as though it had been in the input accretion originally, and hence was designatable by appropriate values of *INPUT*.

Since substituted objects are considered as though they had actually been in the input accretion from the beginning, care must be taken to avoid (the equivalent of) Epimenedes' paradox [G60a]: unbounded resubstitution for the same base object because the object substituted for the base object contains the base object in question. That is, the MSF

$$\langle\!\langle \mathbf{b}_i \rightarrow \mathbf{b}_i \rangle\!\rangle \qquad (5.5)$$

causes an unbounded sequence of substitutions to take place. Such a sequence can take place as well if the MSFs form a cycle.

There are several cases where the interpretation of the substitution MSF, although derivable from the foregoing description, merits some additional comment. Suppose that some input accretion is being parsed, and that the parsing has proceeded to the point where some element of $B(L)$, say b_i, is the first unprocessed base object of the input accretion. Suppose further that for the parsing to continue, the next subtree to be parsed must be headed by the element of $N(L)$ "n_j" (and that it is possible, given b_i, to find such a subtree headed by "n_j"). Let α be an object not containing the base object b_i, and let "n_j" be the operand of the substitution MSF

$$\langle\!\langle \alpha \rightarrow \mathbf{b}_i \rangle\!\rangle \, n_j$$

If the substitution of α for b_i changes the (effective) input accretion in such a way that it becomes impossible to recognize "n_j", then the rule in which "n_j" appears as a metacomponent does not apply, and hence neither does the (particular) MSF in further consideration of the input accretion. This statement generalizes thus: Any modification of the input accretion resulting from a substitution MSF holds only so long as the rule in which the MSF appears is used in the parsing of the (modified) input accretion.

On the other hand, suppose that α in the above MSF were the juxtaposition of two objects $\alpha_h \alpha_t$, and that α_h were recognizable as an "n_j".

In this case, there would be no question as to the applicability of the rule (with respect to this metacomponent). The substitution would therefore be valid, and the object forming α_t would be considered to have been in the input accretion from the beginning; its first base object would be the next base object to be processed by the parsing processor.

All of the questions of interpretation of the substitution MSF can be resolved by remembering that if the substitution is made, the result is as though the substituted object had been in the input accretion from the beginning. On the other hand, if the rule in which the MSF appears turns out not to apply (in the parsing of some particular input accretion) then no substitution MSFs appearing in that rule have any effect on the input accretion.

The Right-Context MSF

Each element of $P(L)$ that appears in the parsing tree of an input accretion may be considered as the head of a subtree whose endpoints form some (connected) portion of the input accretion. (For elements of $B(L)$, the subtree is the endpoint itself.) The parsing processor of Chapter 4 only reexamined a base object from the input accretion if it became necessary to reparse because an alternative rule was being tried.

The right-context MSF allows the input accretion to be rescanned at will, rather than only when an error has occurred. This MSF is symbolized by a suffixed

$$\text{«right-context»} \tag{5.6}$$

As a simple example of the use of this MSF, consider the Algol assignment statement

$$A := 0; \tag{5.7}$$

Some machines have a special instruction which stores a zero value in memory, and the use of such an instruction would produce a more efficient running code than fetching a constant and then storing it. This particular type of assignment statement can be recognized by the rules*

$$0 ; \langle\text{zero}\rangle \tag{5.8}$$
$$\langle\text{left-part list}\rangle \langle\text{zero}\rangle \text{«right-context»}$$
$$\langle\text{arithmetic expression}\rangle \langle\text{assignment statement}\rangle \tag{5.9}$$

---

* Alternatively, the rule
          $\langle$left-part list$\rangle$ 0; «right-context» $\langle$assignment statement$\rangle$
may be used. It is more practical, but a poorer example.

The MSF may be interpreted as a command to begin the scanning of the input accretion for the metacomponent *following* it at the same point at which the scanning for the operand itself began. Hence, in 5.8 and 5.9, the scanning for ⟨zero⟩ and ⟨arithmetic expression⟩ are to begin at exactly the same place in the input accretion. The MSF is a constraint on the left-hand base object of the endpoints of a subtree, and nothing else. In the rule

$$\text{a} \quad \texttt{«right-context»} \quad \text{b} \quad \texttt{«right-context»} \quad \text{c} \quad \text{d} \quad \text{e} \qquad (5.10)$$

the scanning for metacomponents "a", "b", and "c" all begin at the same base object in the input accretion, and the scan for "d" begins at the first base object not used in recognizing the "c". Schematically,

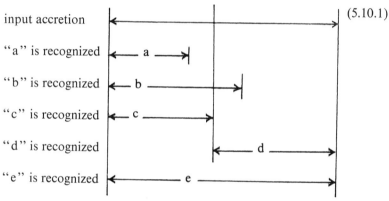

(5.10.1)

The particular number of base objects from the input accretion that are used in recognizing "a" and "b" are of no significance. In 5.10.1, "a" happens to require fewer (and "b", more) base objects than does the metacomponent "c". The significant thing is that the scanning to recognize the "c" begins at the same place that the scanning for "a" and "b" began, and that it is the number of base objects that enter into the "c" that determines where scanning for the "d" begins.

The implementation of the right-context MSF (in the sense of Chapter 4) is particularly simple. All that is required is a test in the recovery section of the parsing processor, in the box just prior to connector 6. The interrogation is made before *INPUT* is lost, and if a right-context MSF appears following the metacomponent that has just been recognized, the list *INPUT* is restored rather than lost.

Because of the implementation for the next MSF to be discussed, it is required that if a right-context MSF appears, it be the right-most suffixed MSF. This is clearly without loss of generality, since the appearance of more than one right-context MSF is of no more significance than the appearance of exactly one.

An operator which allows the specification of a left context in the same way in which the right-context MSF allows specification of the right context has been mentioned in the literature [I62]. This has the disadvantage of requiring that the parsing processor have duplicate sets of tables available to it so that it can scan the input accretion in either direction. While this is not an insurmountable objection, the complexity of the resulting processor seems to outweigh the benefits of having such an operator available in the metasyntactic language.

The Class-Instance MSF

In Chapter 1 an object was defined as "a mark which denotes itself or the class of marks similar to itself". It is sometimes necessary to detect the fact that several objects appearing in some input accretion belong to the same class; in other words, that some number of objects in the accretion are not distinguishable from one another when considered out of the context of the accretion in which they occur. In this limited sense, the objects may be considered as being the "same" as each other. More formally, two objects which are the "same" as each other may be considered to be *instances* of the same *class* of objects. Associated with such a class is a *class-indicator* which is the archetype of the instances of the class, and a *class-name* by which the class is referred to.

For example, in the accretion

$$\textsf{w o p t r q i b w m n t v e g z w x c p}$$

there are three **w**s; more formally, there are three instances of a class whose class-indicator is **w** and whose class name is "the letter **w**".

Certain programming languages require, as a language constraint, that some specific number of instances of the same class appear in the input accretion. As an example, Fortran [I57] has a construction known as a "DO-loop" which is of the form

$$\text{DO} \quad n \quad i = a,b,c$$
$$\text{(sequence of statements)}$$
$$n \quad \text{(statement)} \tag{5.11}$$

in which "n" stands for an integer known as a "statement label". As suggested by 5.11, the "n" following the "DO" and the "n" preceding the terminal statement must be instances of the same class (informally, must be the "same" integer).

A method of denoting this "sameness" in the syntax was proposed by Yershov [Y61b] [Y63]. Certain instances of an element of N(L) occurring in a rule were surrounded with the special brackets " $\langle$ " and " $\rangle$ "; these metacomponents were thereby constrained not only to be heads of sub-trees with the same structure (since the heads were the same elements of N(L)) but also to have the same accretion of endpoints. If the same element of N(L) were to appear in the rule but not enclosed in the special brackets, no constraints were imposed on its recognition. As an example, in the rule

$$\langle a \rangle \quad b \quad a \quad c \quad \langle a \rangle \quad d$$

the subtrees (including endpoints) headed by the first and last "a" are constrained to be instances of the same class, while the middle "a" is not constrained.

Another approach [R62] permitted a limited sort of cross-referencing between rules in the parsing tree of a particular accretion. If a rule r_k is used in the parsing of some accretion, and if this rule has a metacomponent (among others) n_j, then the rule r_j which defines n_j may also access metacomponents to the left of n_j in r_k. Such a cross-reference is an indication that a subtree which is an instance of the same class as the subtree headed by the metacomponent referred to must be recognized at the point of the cross-reference.

These two approaches have in common the requirement that the parsing tree, as well as the accretion formed by the endpoints, be constrained. In what follows, the MSFs that are introduced must be understood to be functions on the endpoints of the subtree, and completely independent of the structure of the subtree. This has the advantage of separating the functions of the endpoints from the functions of the tree structure, which are already completely specifiable by the grammar.

Two MSFs will be used to indicate that the endpoints of some subtree must be the same as the endpoints of some other subtree. A suffixed

$$\text{«class i»} \tag{5.12}$$

indicates that «class i» is to be considered the class-name whose class-instance is the accretion formed by the endpoints of the subtree headed by the operand of the MSF. Similarly, a suffixed

$$\text{«instance i»} \qquad (5.13)$$

indicates that the metacomponent which is the operand of the MSF is not to be considered as recognized unless the endpoints of the subtree which it heads, considered as an accretion, are also an instance of the class whose class-name is «class i».

In both 5.12 and 5.13, the "i" denotes an arbitrary integer, and 5.12, for example, must be considered an abbreviation for the set

«class 1»
«class 2»
«class 3»
. . .

It is these latter MSFs which will appear in the syntax, rather than 5.12 as written.

If more than one class MSF is encountered operating on the same operand, each of the MSFs is considered to be a different class-name for the class-instance formed by the endpoints of the subtree headed by the operand. If more than one instance MSF is encountered operating on the same operand, the metacomponent is considered to be recognized if the endpoints of its subtree are an instance of at least one of the classes indicated by the MSFs.

As an example of the use of the class and instance MSFs, consider the rule of syntax which might be used for the recognition of the structure shown in 5.11:

$$\text{DO } \langle\text{integer}\rangle \text{ «class 1» } \langle\text{increment part}\rangle \langle\text{statement list}\rangle$$
$$\langle\text{integer}\rangle \text{ «instance 1» } \langle\text{statement}\rangle \langle\text{DO-structure}\rangle \qquad (5.14)$$

Because of the class MSF postfixed to the first $\langle\text{integer}\rangle$ in 5.14, the endpoints of the subtree which it heads become the class-instance of the class whose class-name is «class 1». The «instance 1» postfixed to the second $\langle\text{integer}\rangle$ then requires that the endpoints of *that* subtree also be an instance of the class whose class-name is «class 1»; that is, that the integers recognized be "the same".

The class and instance MSFs can be implemented with the same list

(*SUBSTITUTION*) that was used to implement the substitution MSF. The list is controlled as described in that section with the two additions:

(e) When a class MSF is encountered, the MSF is placed in the head of *SUBSTITUTION,* the list is preserved, the object representing the endpoints of the subtree (considered as an accretion) is placed in the head of *SUBSTITUTION,* and the list is again preserved.

(f) When an instance MSF is encountered, the list *SUBSTITU-TION* is scanned backwards (as described under the substitution MSF) to locate the most recent entry of the class whose instance MSF initiated the scan. The operand of the instance MSF is not considered as being recognized unless a match is found between the endpoints of the tree which it heads and the class-instance associated with the class MSF.

Any object which is entered into *SUBSTITUTION* as a consequence of a class MSF, and any object compared therewith as a consequence of an instance MSF, must take into account any substitution MSFs which were applied in the process of recognizing the metacomponent which heads the subtree.

A Problem and Its Solution

One of the reasons for introducing the class and instance MSFs was the desirability of being able to recognize syntactically the DO-structure of 5.11 or 5.14. Unfortunately (for this purpose) when Fortran was first introduced, the definition of the DO-structure was a DO-statement (the first line of 5.11) followed by an arbitrary sequence of statements, followed by a statement whose statement label was the same as the one which appeared in the DO-statement. Although this definition is equivalent to 5.14 in the simple case, it allows several DO-statements to terminate on the same labeled statement:

$$DO \quad n \quad i = a,b,c$$
$$. . .$$
$$DO \quad n \quad j = d,e,f$$
$$. . .$$
$$n \quad (statement) \qquad (5.15)$$

In other words, the DO-statement was a kind of opening parenthesis, but several of these opening parentheses could be terminated by the same closing parenthesis (the labeled statement). The desired pairing was indicated by the statement label.

The syntax which recognizes this peculiar type of pairing requires three rules:

> DO ⟨integer⟩ «class 1» ⟨increment part⟩
> ⟨closing statement list⟩ ⟨DO-structure⟩   (5.16)

> ⟨statement list⟩ DO ⟨integer⟩ «instance 1» ⟨increment part⟩
> ⟨closing statement list⟩ ⟨closing statement list⟩   (5.17)

> ⟨statement list⟩ ⟨integer⟩ «instance 1»
> ⟨statement⟩ ⟨closing statement list⟩   (5.17)

(Not shown are the allowance for a statement label being associated with the DO of 5.16 or 5.17 and the fact that a ⟨DO-structure⟩ is permitted in a ⟨statement list⟩.)

The use of the class and instance MSFs illustrated by the above three rules is dependent on the way in which these MSFs are implemented (described above). Since the MSFs involved are postfixed, they are not interpreted until after their operands have been recognized. If the operands are not recognized at all, an error exit is taken (see Chapter 4) before the MSFs are interpreted. If the operands *are* recognized, the list *SUBSTITUTION* will have been restored prior to any entry being made in it on behalf of a class MSF, and prior to the list being scanned on behalf of an instance MSF. As a result, once a class MSF has made an entry, the entry is available to all instance MSFs in subtrees headed by any metacomponent to the right of the class MSF in the rule in which the MSF occurs.

Since the list *SUBSTITUTION* is scanned from newest entry to oldest, it is possible for a given class to be redefined; this allows (among other things) a ⟨DO-structure⟩ to be one of the elements of a ⟨statement list⟩. The class named «class 1» is temporarily redefined while the inner ⟨DO-structure⟩ is being recognized; when the recognition is completed, the second definition of «class 1» is removed from *SUBSTITUTION* and the original definition is again available.

CHAPTER 6

The Metasemantic and Metapragmatic Language

The basis of any translation technique which is not a word-for-word transcription is the attribution of information content to the structure of the accretion which is provided as input to the translation process. In the traditional translation processes (regardless of the language of the input accretion), this structural information was assumed, but never made explicitly available.

Chapters 3 and 4 of this book discussed a method and a language for making explicit the structure of an input accretion, in a form suitable for further processing. This was accomplished by specifying a set of rules of a language and requiring that any grammatical input accretion in that language be parsable according to those rules. For the set of rules to be complete, it must necessarily include (in some manner) all of the permissible endpoints (that is, the vocabulary of the language) as well as all of the permissible ways in which these endpoints may be combined; hence, parsing according to such a set of rules results in portraying both the vocabulary and the grammar of the input accretion in a form suitable for further processing.

The missing (and important!) link is the meaning that is to be attributed to this structure. This chapter specifies a language in which a meaning, in terms of the generation of an accretion, can be attributed to each of a set of rules in the environment of the parsing tree of some particular input accretion.

A rule of semantics was defined as the means by which a meaning is attributed to an object to make it a symbol; similarly, a rule of pragmatics was defined as the means by which a single meaning is selected when more than one had been attributed to a symbol. One of the problems in describing the semantics and pragmatics of a language is the (present) lack of precision in these notions of attribution and selection. This problem is reflected in the metasemantic and metapragmatic language; the metalanguage itself can be specified precisely, but its use to specify the semantics and pragmatics of a source language is an art and not a science. As a consequence, the metasemantic and metapragmatic language will be introduced in a somewhat less formal manner than was the metasyntactic language.

The Basic Form of the Construct

The set of rules which form the grammar of a language comprise the first of the two additional inputs of Fig. 1.3 which distinguish a syntax-oriented translator from a conventional translator. In Chapter 2 it was pointed out that with each rule there is associated a *construct* which specifies (in some manner) the objects to be placed in the output accretion if the rule was used in parsing the input accretion. The set of these constructs forms the remaining additional input shown in Fig. 1.3.

A construct is an accretion of a particular type (to be described in the remainder of this chapter) which is enclosed in the braces "{" and "}". These braces are not a part of the construct, and serve only to delimit it.

The base objects forming the accretion are of two types: those to which no meaning has been attributed (*pure objects*) and those to which a meaning has been given (*symbols*). The pure objects will be printed in the same boldface sans serif type that was used for the elements of $\mathbf{B}(L)$; they are not interpreted by the unparsing processor, but are merely written into the output accretion at the time that the unparsing processor encounters them. The symbols, on the other hand, will be printed in a normal type face; their meanings are attributed to them by the unparsing processor.

The most rudimentary construct consists of the null object between braces: {}. Next simplest are constructs whose accretions consist solely of pure objects; as examples, consider the constructs associated with the first five rules of 2.8:

$$\{\textbf{A}\} \quad \{\textbf{B}\} \quad \{\textbf{C}\} \quad \{\textbf{D}\} \quad \{\textbf{E}\}$$

These five constructs, when interpreted by the unparsing processor, will cause the base objects **A, B, C, D**, and **E**, respectively, to be placed in the output accretion.

These basic constructs suffice to specify the semantics and pragmatics of the rules of Fig. 3.29 which define ⟨letter⟩ and ⟨digit⟩. These thirty-six rules, and their associated constructs, may be abbreviated

$$
\begin{array}{llll}
\textbf{A} & \langle\text{letter}\rangle & \{\textbf{A}\} & [1] \\
& \cdots \\
\textbf{Z} & \langle\text{letter}\rangle & \{\textbf{Z}\} & [26] \\
\textbf{0} & \langle\text{digit}\rangle & \{\textbf{0}\} & [27] \\
& \cdots \\
\textbf{9} & \langle\text{digit}\rangle & \{\textbf{9}\} & [36]
\end{array}
$$

where the rule numbers have (again) been written to the right of the rules (and their constructs) in square brackets. The meaning which is attributed to the appearance of the base objects **A**, ..., **9** in the input accretion, therefore, is the placing of the corresponding base object into the output accretion.

From One Construct to Another

The simple constructs of the preceding section are *terminal* constructs; if the processing of one of them is started by the unparsing processor, it is completed without interruption, and in particular, without processing another construct.

Since the purpose of the constructs is to specify the objects to be placed in the output accretion in the environment of the parsing tree, it is clear that there must be some provision for a construct to take advantage of its environment.

The environment of a construct is the rule with which it is associated, considered as a subtree of the parsing tree of some input accretion. In this respect, the metaresult of a rule is the head of a subtree, and the metacomponents of the rule which are elements of N(L) are the heads of (lower) subtrees, and hence metaresults of (other) rules. These (other) rules also have constructs associated with them. The obvious way to allow a construct to utilize its environment is to provide a mechanism whereby it can invoke the processing of the constructs associated with the metacomponents (which are elements of N(L)) of the rule with which it is associated. The elements of N(L) in a rule will be numbered from right to left, beginning with the metaresult, which is numbered "0". A reference to the construct associated with a metacomponent (actually, associated with the rule in the parsing tree in which the metacomponent appears as the metaresult) is made by writing the index associated with the metacomponent, enclosed in the brackets "[" and "]". Such a symbol will be called a *clause*; if more than one clause appears in a construct, they will be identified by being referred to by their enclosed numbers, e.g. 3-clause. As an example, the last rule of 2.8, with its associated construct, is:

$$\langle variable \rangle = \langle expression \rangle \langle statement \rangle \ \{[1]S[2]\}$$

in which the 1-clause refers to the construct associated with $\langle expression \rangle$ in its appearance as a metaresult, and the 2-clause refers, similarly, to $\langle variable \rangle$.

The *ad hoc* introduction of links in the output of the parsing processor (see Chapter 4) may now be explained. If the output of the parsing processor is written from top to bottom (rather than from left to right), then, e.g., the result of parsing the accretion "$A = B + C + D$" becomes (from 4.8)

1:	3	{**C**}	(6.1)
2:	4	{**D**}	
3:	8	{[2]**A**[1]}	
4:	−2		
5:	8	{[2]**A**[1]}	
6:	−1		
7:	7	{**L**[1]}	
8:	2	{**B**}	
9:	6	{[1]**S**[2]}	
10:	−3		
11:	1	{**A**}	
12:	−9		

in which row numbers have been added on the left and the construct associated with the rules have been written out on the right. A careful examination of 6.1 will show that in the context of the output of the parsing processor, a k-clause (referring, in the context of a rule, to the kth element of N(L), counting from the right, appearing in the rule) refers to the kth line below the construct.

As is also apparent from 6.1, there is no restriction on the sequence in which the clauses appear in a construct, compared with the meta-components to which they refer. For example, in the construct written on row 3, the 2-clause comes first, followed by the 1-clause, while the converse is true of the construct on row 9. There is an even greater degree of freedom: it is possible for the same clause to occur more than once in the same construct. Hence, the construct

$$\{[1][3][1][2][1]\}$$

is an allowable one, were a use to be found for it.

Constructs containing clauses and pure objects can be used to specify the sequence in which other constructs are to be manipulated and to provide objects to be placed into the output accretion. As a simple example, when an identifier (composed, according to the rules of Fig. 3.29, of an accretion of letters) is found in the input accretion, it may be desirable to reproduce the identifier in the output accretion. The rules and their associated constructs for the recognition of the individual letters were given at the end of the preceding section. Now, by the rules for the construction of an identifier, a single letter is clearly an identifier:

$$\langle\text{letter}\rangle \langle\text{identifier}\rangle \{[1]\} [57]$$

and an ⟨identifier⟩ with a ⟨letter⟩ juxtaposed on the right is also an ⟨identifier⟩:

$$\langle\text{identifier}\rangle \langle\text{letter}\rangle \langle\text{identifier}\rangle \{[2][1]\} [55]$$

In summary, a clause is a way of placing into the output accretion whatever objects are required as a consequence of having recognized (in the input accretion) a subtree headed by the element of N(L) to which the clause points. In this light, the construct for Rule 60 of Fig. 3.29 becomes clear:

$$\langle\text{left-part list}\rangle \langle\text{arithmetic expression}\rangle$$
$$\langle\text{assignment statement}\rangle \{[1][2]\} [60]$$

The assembly-language coding which (when executed) will evaluate the arithmetic expression is placed into the output accretion, followed by the coding which will cause this value to be stored into the memory locations referred to (symbolically) in the left-part list.

Punctuation Marks and Format Control

The output accretion can be considered as a single object, and is generated by placing base objects into it one at a time. For use by human beings, and for some further uses by machines, this is not the most convenient format.

In the context of a procedure-oriented language being translated into an assembly language, the format of the output must conform to the requirements imposed by the further processing of the assembly languages. Most assembly languages have a very simple form:

(a) A *program* in such a language consists of a sequence of *lines* written one under another;

(b) Each *line* contains one or more *lists*, written on the line from left to right; and

(c) The left-hand list is used to indicate the (symbolic) location of the line, the next list is used to indicate the operator associated with the line, and the remaining lists (if any) are the operands for the operator [G65b].

These characteristics suggest that the metapragmatic language must have a way of indicating the beginning of a new line and a way of indicating a new list on a line. In actual practice, the left-hand list is usually empty, since most lines do not require a symbolic location indication.

Punctuation marks will be indicated in constructs by characters from a special alphabet (special in the sense of distinct and recognizable). As a matter of convenience, the special alphabet chosen for Chapters 6 and 7 is the set $\{\alpha, \beta, \gamma\}$. The interpretation given to these objects when used as punctuation symbols is:

α The first base object following is the first base object of the left-most list of a new line

β The first base object following is the first base object of the second-from-the-left list of a line, and a new line will be started if necessary

γ The first base object following is the first base object of the next available list of a line.

In terms of a typewriter, the punctuation mark "α" is a carriage-return which also spaces the paper vertically. A "β" is a tabulation to the first tab stop; if the carriage is already past the first tab stop, a carriage-return and vertical paper feed is executed followed by the tabulation. A "γ", finally, is merely a tabulation to the next tab stop, wherever it may be. (The assumption is made that the carriage is sufficiently long, so that a carriage-return will not be required unless requested.)

Rule 56 of Fig. 3.29, and its associated construct, are

$$\langle\text{identifier}\rangle \langle\text{primary}\rangle \{\beta\textbf{LDA}\gamma[1]\} \quad [56]$$

Hence, when this rule is invoked in the parsing process, the object placed into the output accretion is the assembly language instruction "**LDA**" (interpreted "load the A register"), followed by the identifier of the cell whose contents are to be loaded. The "**LDA**" is placed into the operation list of a line, because of the punctuation mark "β"; similarly, the identifier is placed into the first available operand list, because of the "γ".

Dummy Variables and Their Replacements

In all of the constructs so far discussed, the objects to be placed into the output accretion either appeared explicitly in a construct or appeared in some other construct referenced by a clause. In other words, for each subtree of a parsing tree (as well, of course, as for the entire tree) it is possible to associate an object which is the result of interpreting the constructs associated with the rules used to form the parsing tree. This object (in the constructs so far discussed) is completely determined by the subtree, and is in no way dependent on the way that the subtree fits into the overall parsing tree.

This assumption of independence is valid when the meaning that is to be attributed by a construct is not dependent on the context in which a rule is used in the parsing. Even with grammars that do not require such features as the right-context MSF (see Chapter 5), the usual case is that the constructs will need to vary the meanings they assign as a function of the position of the subtree in the overall parsing tree. As an example of this, the recognition of the object "$+$" in the language of arithmetic assignment statements is independent of context, although the assignment of meaning to the "$+$" is not, since the "$+$" may be either unary or binary.

The context-dependent assignment of meaning to an object requires two additional features in the metasemantic and metapragmatic language. First, there must be a way of indicating a "dummy" meaning—one which will be provided by the environment in which the subtree is used (in the sense of the entire parsing tree). Second, since it is the clause which causes the processing of the constructs associated with a subtree, there must be a way of indicating in a clause the dummy variables for which a meaning is to be substituted, and also what that meaning is.

Dummy variables will be represented in constructs with the letters from yet another alphabet: {A, ..., Z}. This alphabet is chosen because it does not conflict with the alphabet of punctuation marks ($\{\alpha, \beta, \gamma\}$), the alphabet of objects (boldface sans serif type), and the other meta-linguistic symbols.

Two examples of constructs consisting of nothing but dummy variables are those associated with Rules 37 and 38 from Fig. 3.29:

$$- \langle \text{adding operator} \rangle \; \{s\} \; [37]$$
$$+ \langle \text{adding operator} \rangle \; \{A\} \; [38]$$

In these two cases the meaning is completely context-dependent (that is, there is no meaning except that which is substituted for the dummy variables). The context-dependence of meaning, as pointed out above, is not necessarily related to the context-dependence or context-inde-pendence of the syntax of the language; for the language in which the two above rules appear, the grammar is context-independent.

The meaning that is to be substituted for a dummy variable is provided in the clause which invokes the subtree in which the dummy variable appears. This is done with a *phrase* embedded in the clause. A phrase is formed by a dummy variable followed by some object; the object is to be substituted for the dummy variable. These phrases (as many as desired) are set off by (metalinguistic) commas from the digit which characterizes the clause. As an example, consider Rules 44 and 64 of Fig. 3.29:

$$\langle \text{adding operator} \rangle \; \langle \text{term} \rangle \; \langle \text{unary arithmetic expression} \rangle$$
$$\{[1] \, [2]\} \; [44]$$
$$\langle \text{unary arithmetic expression} \rangle \; \langle \text{arithmetic expression} \rangle$$
$$\{[1, \text{A}, \text{s}\beta\textbf{CHS}]\} \; [64]$$

The effect of the construct associated with Rule 44 is to produce (with the 1-clause) the object associated with ⟨term⟩, followed (because of the 2-clause) by the dummy variable "A" or "s", depending on which of the two possible adding operators occurred in the input accretion. The construct associated with Rule 64 causes this new object to be copied, but with the null object substituted for "A" and the object "βCHS" substituted for "s". If the (purely *ad hoc*) assumption is made that the object associated with ⟨term⟩ represents assembly-language coding which, when executed, will cause some value to be computed and left in an accumulator, and if the object **CHS** is understood to be a "change sign" instruction when executed, then the effect of these constructs is to cause a term to be evaluated and the resulting value to have its sign changed if the term were prefixed with a unary " − ". (A unary " + " is ignored by substituting the null object for "A".)

In the examples given above, only pure objects were illustrated as replacements for dummy variables. It is possible for more involved meanings to be inserted with clauses. For example, a clause may cause the substitution of a phrase which contains within itself another clause:

$$[1, A[2, B\textbf{C}]]$$

and this may be carried on to arbitrary depth. The metapragmatic functions to be discussed in the next two sections may also appear in phrases.

Metasemantic and Metapragmatic Functions (MPFs)

The mechanisms described so far in this chapter allow meanings to be associated with rules in three distinct ways. First, a meaning can be associated directly with a specific rule by a construct which contains nothing but pure objects. Second, a meaning may be associated with an entire subtree headed by a rule; in this case the construct contains clauses (possibly in addition to base objects). The third possibility is for a construct to contain dummy variables; this allows a meaning to be associated with a subtree as a function of the way in which the subtree is used in the overall parsing tree, rather than in an absolute (independent-of-use) sense.

For any particular source language, there may be additional meanings which cannot be specified with these three mechanisms. These fall into two broad categories:

(a) Meanings which are unique to each use of a rule, rather than merely to the rule itself, and

(b) Meanings which are dependent on the particular structure of the parsing tree above some subtree, rather than on the use or non-use of some rule in that structure.

Since such meanings are dependent on the source language, in the same sense that some source languages require the MSFs of Chapter 5 for their grammars, it is not possible to give an exhaustive list. Instead, a few examples will be given, and the general technique described.

For an example of the first class of MPFs, it is necessary to turn to a more complex language than that of assignment statements. The conditional statement of Algol [N63] is conveniently simple. This type of statement exists in several forms; one of these forms has the syntax*

$$\textbf{if}\ \langle \text{Boolean expression}\rangle\ \textbf{then}\ \langle \text{unconditional statement}\rangle$$
$$\textbf{else}\ \langle \text{statement}\rangle\ \langle \text{conditional statement}\rangle$$

The ⟨Boolean expression⟩ is assumed to be the head of a subtree which generates coding which, when executed, leaves a Boolean value (**true** or **false**) in a special register. Both ⟨unconditional statement⟩ and ⟨statement⟩ are assumed to head subtrees which generate some kind of executable coding. This type of conditional statement causes the "unconditional statement" to be executed if the Boolean expression is true, and the "statement" to be executed if the Boolean expression is false. Consequently, the coding generated for the conditional statement must insert unconditional transfer instructions to jump over the coding that is not to be executed. These unconditional transfer instructions must jump to labels which are unique to each use of the above rule, so that the flow of control through the program is the one desired by the programmer.

Two MPFs are used to (respectively) generate a new label and to regenerate a previously generated label. The first of these is symbolized

$$\approx 1$$

which, when encountered, will generate a unique label. The MPF

$$\approx 2n$$

will regenerate the nth preceding label (counting from "0") generated by the "≈ 1" (1-function). The construct associated with the rule in the preceding paragraph is therefore:

$$\textbf{if}\ \langle \text{Be}\rangle\ \textbf{then}\ \langle \text{us}\rangle\ \textbf{else}\ \langle \text{s}\rangle\ \langle \text{cs}\rangle\ \{[3]\beta\, \textbf{J}\textbf{F}\gamma \approx 1[2]\beta\, \textbf{J}\gamma \approx 1\alpha \approx 21[1]\alpha \approx 20\}$$

---

* This rule is actually a combination of parts of two rules from the Algol report [N63, section 4.5.1]. It is correct, but incomplete.

The result of processing this construct yields:

> (coding to evaluate the Boolean expression)
> **JF** label-1
> (coding for unconditional statement)
> **J** label-2
> label-1 (coding for statement)
> label-2 (whatever comes next)

in which **JF** is assumed to be an instruction which will jump if the result of evaluating the Boolean expression is **false**, and **J** is assumed to be an unconditional jump.

Note particularly the 2-function, and the way it regenerates labels. In the example below, the 1-functions and 2-functions are written vertically, and the generated labels listed alongside:

$$\approx 1 \quad \text{label-1}$$
$$\approx 1 \quad \text{label-2}$$
$$\approx 1 \quad \text{label-3}$$
$$\approx 20 \quad \text{label-3}$$
$$\approx 21 \quad \text{label-2}$$
$$\approx 1 \quad \text{label-4}$$
$$\approx 23 \quad \text{label-1}$$
$$\approx 22 \quad \text{label-2}$$
$$\approx 21 \quad \text{label-3}$$
$$\approx 20 \quad \text{label-4}$$

The Other Kind of MPF

The remaining broad category of MPF is one in which the meaning assigned by the MPF is dependent on the structure of the parsing tree above some particular subtree, rather than on the use or non-use of some rule in that structure.

As an example, it is occasionally desirable to know the number of pairs of parentheses surrounding a given operation; one possible reason for doing this is the generation of "safe" places to store temporary results.

Another way of protecting temporary results depends on the use of dummy variables and the way the process of replacing them is implemented. Although the details of the implementation belong in the next chapter, a brief explanation can be given here. Whenever a phrase is encountered in a clause, an entry is made in a list (similar to the list *SUBSTITUTION* used for the substitution MSF). Whenever a dummy variable is found, this list is scanned from most recent entry to least recent, looking for a replacement.

The 3-function is of the form

$$\approx 3\text{D}$$

where "D" is some dummy variable. The value of this function is the number of entries in the replacement list which could replace the specified dummy variable. A simple example is the construct associated with rule 52 of Fig. 3.29:

$\langle$factor$\rangle \uparrow \langle$primary$\rangle \langle$factor$\rangle$
$\{[2]\beta\textbf{STA}\gamma\textbf{T} \approx 3\text{T}[1, \text{T}]\beta\textbf{LDB}\gamma\textbf{T} \approx 3\text{T}\beta\textbf{CALL}\gamma\textbf{EXP}\}$ [52]

The **STA** is a command to store the "A" register, the **LDB** a command to load the "B" register, **CALL** invokes a subroutine, and the **EXP** subroutine expects the base in the "B" register and the exponent in the "A" register. (**EXP** is also assumed to leave its result in the "A" register.) Suppose that there are k replacements for the dummy variable "T" at the time this construct is processed. This will cause the generation of "Tk" as the symbolic address of the temporary storage location which is used as the operand of the **STA** and **LDB** instructions. Any temporary storage locations which are required in the coding generated by the 1-clause (and, of course, which are generated by the same mechanism) will have a value for the 3-function which is at least 1 greater, because of the T-phrase in the 1-clause. This guarantees that the contents of the temporary storage location will be "safe" during the computation resulting from executing the coding generated by the 1-clause.

The General MPF

The general form of the MPF is the symbol "$\approx$" followed by an object. The first base object following the "$\approx$" is used to determine which particular subprocessor will be invoked, and the remaining base objects (if any) are the operands for the function. The number of base objects which serve as operands is determined by the particular subprocessor (and function) invoked; the 1-function has no operands, while the 2-function and 3-function have one operand.

Since both the number of base objects in the argument vector and their interpretation depend entirely on the particular function that is invoked, it is convenient to consider the "$\approx$" as being an escape character from the language in which the constructs are written into some other language. This other language is not within the province of this book and (except for the examples given in the preceding sections) will not be discussed.

The number of different MPFs and their meanings are limited only by the ingenuity of a programmer and the requirements of the language being translated. In particular, several translation schemes (e.g. [D61a] and [R64]) have made extensive use of push-down lists; these schemes can be used in the parsing-unparsing structure by providing MPFs which manipulate private push-down lists in particular ways, independently of the lists used in the unparsing processor.

Constructs Which Write Syntax

One of the ways in which the "power" of a procedure-oriented language can be increased is to include certain metalinguistic capabilities in the language itself. Examples of this are the declarations of arithmetic type found in Algol [N63] and the later versions of Fortran [A64a].* In the translation of such languages, the output of the unparsing processor cannot be assembly language coding, since not all of the metalinguistic information is available during the translation process. Languages of this type require (at least) an additional pass through the entire translation process, but one in which the output of the unparsing processor is a new set of additional inputs to the parsing processor, rather than assembly language coding [I63].

In order for a translation process to be able to be iterated, it is necessary for a construct to be able to generate rules of syntax, each with its own associated construct. As an illustration, consider the Algol declaration

real p, q, r;

which has the interpretation that the identifiers **p**, **q**, and **r** are to be considered as having values with arithmetic type **real** associated with them. This declaration (as are many of the other declarations of Algol)

---

* The original specifications for Fortran also contained a type declaration [I55] as well as some other features which were apparently never implemented [I54].

is metalinguistic; the first iteration of the translation process must effect the inclusion of rules and constructs of the form [I61d] [I63a]:

$$\textbf{p} \ \langle\text{real simple variable}\rangle \ \{\textbf{p}\}$$

in the syntax used for the second iteration, so that the identifiers **p**, **q**, and **r** may be recognized as having been declared as identifiers of type **real.**

A construct which is to generate syntax must contain a construct within itself.* This inner construct must be delimited by the braces "{" and "}", to delimit the inner construct from the outer. These braces, in addition to delimiting the inner construct *per se*, also delimit the interpretation of the metalanguage commands (such as clauses and MPFs) which are in the inner construct; normally, anything in a construct which is enclosed in braces is not interpreted. (Remember that the definition of a construct was an accretion enclosed in braces, but that the braces were *not* a part of the construct.)

In order for constructs to generate syntax of the form required for the type declaration given as an example above, it is necessary that an additional mechanism be introduced which allows the interpretation of certain symbols which are in embedded constructs. This is indicated by the prefixed unary operator "!", which indicates that the interpretation of the clause or MPF which follows it is to be as though the clause or MPF were outside one pair of braces; more than one "!" may be prefixed to a clause or MPF, providing that no more "!"s are prefixed than there are embracing braces.

With this additional operator in the metalanguage, it is possible to write the rules and constructs which can be used to parse the declaration and produce the syntax given above:

$$\langle\text{letter}\rangle \ \langle\text{identifier}\rangle \ \{[1]\}$$
$$\langle\text{identifier}\rangle \ \langle\text{letter}\rangle \ \langle\text{identifier}\rangle \ \{[2]\,[1]\}$$
$$\langle\text{identifier}\rangle \ \langle\text{identifier list}\rangle \ \{\alpha[1]\beta{\scriptstyle B}\gamma\{![1]\}\}$$
$$\langle\text{identifier list}\rangle, \ \langle\text{identifier}\rangle \ \langle\text{identifier list}\rangle$$
$$\{[2]\alpha[1]\beta{\scriptstyle B}\gamma\{![1]\}\}$$
$$\textbf{real} \ \langle\text{identifier list}\rangle; \ \langle\text{real declaration}\rangle$$
$$\{[1,{\scriptstyle B} \ \langle\text{real simple variable}\rangle]\}$$

---

* A construct which generates syntax generates a rule with its associated construct, which latter must therefore have been embedded.

Substitution of other rules for the last one given above would allow the recognition of other declarations, and the generation of the appropriate syntax:

$$\textbf{integer} \langle \text{identifier list} \rangle; \langle \text{integer declaration} \rangle$$
$$\{[1, \text{B} \langle \text{integer simple variable} \rangle]\}$$

The Constructs for Assignment Statements

Writing constructs to produce the mapping of a procedure-oriented language into an assembly language requires a number of assumptions. These assumptions fall into two general classes: first, the assumptions which concern themselves with the syntax of the assembly language and the capabilities of the target machine; and second, the assumptions which are strictly *ad hoc*, but which provide, e.g., the sort of inheritable properties discussed in brief in Chapter 2.

A number of assumptions of the first type have been made in previous sections of this chapter, when the rules from Fig. 3.29 were used as examples. Together with some additional assumptions, they are listed here:

(a) The target machine is assumed to have two working registers, the "A" register and the "B" register

(b) The symbolic operation codes, together with their meanings, are

$$
\begin{array}{ll}
\textbf{MPY } m & (m) \times (A) \to A \\
\textbf{DIV } m & (m) \div (A) \to A \\
\textbf{STO } m & (A) \to m \\
\textbf{ADD } m & (m) + (A) \to A \\
\textbf{SUB } m & (m) - (A) \to A \\
\textbf{LDB } m & (m) \to B \\
\textbf{LDA } m & (m) \to A \\
\textbf{CHS} & -(A) \to A
\end{array}
$$

(Note the operations **DIV** and **SUB**; they are "reversed" arithmetic operations [B60a] [I60].)

(c) The assembler has a library, and a routine from the library may be evoked with the **CALL** operation, followed by the name of the desired routine. The routine **EXP** is an exponentiation routine which expects the exponent in the A-register and the base in the B-register; the result is left in the A-register

A	l	{**A**}	[1]		$-$	ao	{s}	[37]
B	l	{**B**}	[2]		$+$	ao	{A}	[38]
C	l	{**C**}	[3]		$*$	mo	{**MPY**}	[39]
D	l	{**D**}	[4]		$/$	mo	{**DIV**}	[40]
E	l	{**E**}	[5]		${}_{10}$	in	ep	{${}_{10}$[1]}	[41]
F	l	{**F**}	[6]		**.**	ui	df	{**.**[1]}	[42]
G	l	{**G**}	[7]		**(**	ae	**)** p	{[1,т]}	[43]
H	l	{**H**}	[8]		ao	t	uae	{[1][2]}	[44]
I	l	{**I**}	[9]		ao	ui	in	{[2,A$+$,s$-$][1]}	[45]
J	l	{**J**}	[10]		ae	uae	ae	{[2]β**STO**γ**T**$\approx$3т[1,Aβ**ADD**γ**T**$\approx$3т, sβ**SUB**γ**T**$\approx$3т,т]}	[46]
K	l	{**K**}	[11]		df	dn	{**0**[1]}	[47]
L	l	{**L**}	[12]		dn	ep	un	{[2][1]}	[48]
M	l	{**M**}	[13]		dn	un	{[1]${}_{10}$$+$**1**}	[49]
N	l	{**N**}	[14]		d	ui	{[1]	[50]
O	l	{**O**}	[15]		ep	un	{**1.0**[1]}	[51]
P	l	{**P**}	[16]		f	↑	p f	{[2]β**STO**γ**T**$\approx$3т[1,т]β**LDB**γ**T**$\approx$3т β**CALL**γ**EXP**}	[52]
Q	l	{**Q**}	[17]		f	t	{[1]}	[53]
R	l	{**R**}	[18]		id	=	lp	{β**STO**γ[1]}	[54]
S	l	{**S**}	[19]		id	l	id	{[2][1]}	[55]
T	l	{**T**}	[20]		id	p	{β**LDA**γ[1]}	[56]
U	l	{**U**}	[21]		l	id	{[1]}	[57]
V	l	{**V**}	[22]		lp	lpl	{[1]}	[58]
W	l	{**W**}	[23]		lpl	lp	lpl	{[2][1]}	[59]
X	l	{**X**}	[24]		lpl	ae	as	{[1][2]}	[60]
Y	l	{**Y**}	[25]		p	f	{[1]}	[61]
Z	l	{**Z**}	[26]		t	mo	f t	{[3]β**STO**γ**T**$\approx$3т[1,т]β[2]γ**T**$\approx$3т}	[62]
0	d	{**0**}	[27]		t	ae	{[1]}	[63]
1	d	{**1**}	[28]		uae	ae	{[1,A,sβ**CHS**]}	[64]
2	d	{**2**}	[29]		un	p	{β**LDA**γ(**[1]**)}	[65]
3	d	{**3**}	[30]		ui	d	ui	{[2][1]}	[66]
4	d	{**4**}	[31]		ui	df	dn	{[2][1]}	[67]
5	d	{**5**}	[32]		ui	dn	{[1]**.0**}	[68]
6	d	{**6**}	[33]		ui	in	{$+$[1]}	[69]
7	d	{**7**}	[34]					
8	d	{**8**}	[35]					
9	d	{**9**}	[36]					

FIG. 6.2

(d) All numbers must be represented in the form

$$a.b_{10}c$$

and will be converted by the assembler to its internal representation

(e) If a number is enclosed in parentheses and then used as an operand, the actual operand will be the address of the location in which the assembly system has placed the value of the number represented. (In other words, a literal facility is provided [I61] [R62a].)

The only assumption of the second type (that is not clearly a result of one of the assumptions of the first type) is that the coding generated by ⟨primary⟩, ⟨factor⟩, ⟨term⟩, ⟨unary arithmetic expression⟩, and ⟨arithmetic expression⟩ will, when it is executed, leave a value in the A-register.

Figure 6.2 displays the grammar of assignment statements, together with the constructs associated with each of the rules. The reader is advised to examine this figure carefully; as an exercise, the conversion of numbers in the representations permitted by the syntax to the single representation permitted in the output accretion should be worked out.

Multiple Constructs and the 0-clause

There are a number of situations where it may be desirable to have more than one output produced as a result of the unparsing process. As a common example, it may be desirable to produce not only an output which is acceptable to an assembly program for further processing, but also to produce a printer listing which shows the coding generated for each of the source language statements.

One way of solving this problem is to have multiple constructs associated with each rule. It is convenient (for reasons to be discussed in a moment) to make the left-most construct the one which generates assembly output, and the next left-most construct the one which generates printer listings. No particular use has been found for more than these two constructs, but the processing method is a general one.

In a situation where multiple constructs are used, it is possible to give a meaning to the 0-clause, at least when it occurs in other than the left-most construct of a rule. Earlier in this chapter it was pointed out that an n-clause (for $n > 0$) causes the interpretation of another construct; to be precise, it causes the interpretation of the construct associated with the nth metacomponent which is an element of $N(L)$ in a particular rule, from the rule where that n^{th} metacomponent was defined (in this parsing) as a metaresult.

The interpretation of the 0-clause is similar; it causes the interpretation of the construct written to the left of the construct in which it occurs. This allows the printer-listing construct to reference certain subtrees of the assembly-generating constructs, at places where entire statements have been recreated on the printer listing, for the purpose of including the generated assembly coding as a part of the documentation.

CHAPTER 7

Details of an Unparsing Processor

This chapter gives the details of a typical unparsing processor for the metasemantic and metapragmatic language of Chapter 6. This processor requires two inputs:

(a) The output of the parsing processor, as described in Chapter 4, and

(b) The table of constructs associated with the rules.

In addition to the output of the parsing processor, the last cell in the output (which contains a link to the head of the parsing tree) must itself be indicated. The output of the parsing processor is considered as a vector identified by the symbol PARSE, and the symbol k has, as its initial value, the cell number of this final link.

The table of constructs (which form the second additional input to the translator of Fig. 1.3) is arranged in a matrix identified by the symbol MATRIX. The rule number of the rule with which the construct is associated is the row number of the matrix, and each constituent object or symbol in the construct occupies a column in that row. The leading "{" is uniformly eliminated; for the constructs of 2.8, repeated here with row numbers,

$$[1] \quad \{\mathbf{A}\}$$
$$[2] \quad \{\mathbf{B}\}$$
$$[3] \quad \{\mathbf{C}\}$$
$$[4] \quad \{\mathbf{D}\}$$
$$[5] \quad \{\mathbf{E}\}$$
$$[6] \quad \{\mathbf{L}[1]\}$$
$$[7] \quad \{[2]\mathbf{A}[1]\}$$
$$[8] \quad \{[1]\mathbf{S}[2]\}$$

the corresponding matrix is:

```
A }
B }
C }
D }
E }
L [ 1 ]   }
  [ 2 ] A [ 1 ] }
  [ 1 ] S [ 2 ] }
```

The output of the unparsing processor is produced object-at-a-time. Only pure objects and punctuation marks are transmitted toward the output accretion. The pure objects are placed in the output accretion; the punctuation marks may actually evoke some kind of control action, but these details are not shown in the flow charts.

Further Comments on MATRIX

The positive-numbered rows of MATRIX contain the constructs provided with the rules. It is convenient to use the negative-numbered rows to provide storage for the substitutions for dummy variables. In these rows the first four columns are preempted for some additional information required in substituting for dummy variables, and the substitution itself starts in column 5. A "}" is generated at the end of each substitution.

Column 1 is a number indicating the first unused column in the row
(the column to the right of the "}");
Column 2 is the dummy variable for which this row may substitute;
Column 3 indicates how far from the head of the parsing tree the
unparsing was at the time this row was entered into MATRIX;
and
Column 4 indicates the cell number in the vector PARSE that points
to the construct that was processed which caused this row to be
entered.

An entry is made into a negative row of MATRIX for each phrase that is encountered in a clause. Since these phrases may themselves contain clauses, etc., column 4 is required so that when the substitution is taking place, the appropriate link will be found in PARSE. Also, substitutions in a clause apply only to those constructs processed as a result of the clause. Hence, if a substitution contains a phrase, that phrase must be processed as though it were at the original level; column 3 is used to control this.

The Lists Used in Unparsing

There are six lists (see Chapter 4) used in the unparsing processor. They are *INSIDE, ROW, COLUMN, LEVEL, COUNT,* and *NEGATIVE.* These six lists are all preserved and restored at the same time, and none of them is ever lost.

> *INSIDE* is initially set to zero. It counts the number of "{" that have occurred inside a construct, and is used only when a construct with its surrounding braces appears inside another construct.
>
> *ROW* indicates the row of MATRIX that is currently being processed.
>
> *COLUMN*, similarly, indicates the column of MATRIX that is currently being processed.
>
> *LEVEL* is initially set to zero. It indicates the number of constructs intervening between the construct currently being processed and the head of the parsing tree. When its value is restored to zero, the unparsing is completed.
>
> *COUNT* is the pointer to the cell of PARSE which points to the current value of *ROW*.
>
> *NEGATIVE* is initially set to zero. It is decremented by one each time a substitution is entered into a negative-numbered row of MATRIX.

In addition to these lists, there are a number of symbols with which single values are associated.

> p is initially set to zero, and is used to count "[" and "]" when clauses are being copied into MATRIX for later processing.
>
> t is initially set to zero. It is used to count the "!"'s when copying constructs that are within constructs, in order to determine whether a following clause or MPF should be interpreted, rather than copied.
>
> k initially points to the last value of the vector PARSE, and is used to point to other values in PARSE as the need arises.

OUTPUT is set to "1" when objects are to be written into the output
accretion, and to "0" when objects are to be written into a row
of MATRIX.

CHARACTER holds the object currently being processed, other
than a pure object or punctuation mark.

The locations TEMP, T2, and T3 are temporary storage locations.

Subroutines

As is customary in all programs, a number of subprocesses have been
identified, isolated, and formed into subroutines. These subroutines have

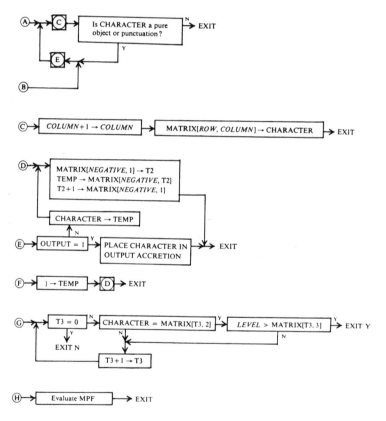

FIG. 7.1

been given arbitrary designations (the letters "A" through "H"). They are flow-charted in Fig. 7.1.

Subroutine "A" scans the current row of MATRIX. Pure objects and punctuation marks are written either to the output accretion (if the value of OUTPUT is 1) or to one of the negative-numbered rows of MATRIX (if the value of OUTPUT is 0). When exit is made from Subroutine "A", the first symbol encountered which was not a pure object nor a punctuation mark has been left in CHARACTER for further processing.

Subroutine "B" is the same as Subroutine "A" except that the object in CHARACTER on entry to Subroutine "B" is written out before the current row of MATRIX is scanned further.

Subroutine "C" actually gets the objects from MATRIX. It first increments *COLUMN*, and then moves an object from MATRIX[*ROW*, *COLUMN*] to CHARACTER.

Subroutine "D" places the object in TEMP into the next free column of negative-numbered row "q" of MATRIX. MATRIX[q, 1] is then incremented to indicate that the column has been used.

Subroutine "E" tests the value of OUTPUT to determine whether the object in CHARACTER should be written into the output accretion or into a negative-numbered row of MATRIX. If the latter, Subroutine "D" is invoked.

Subroutine "F" is used to write a "}" as the final (significant) object of a negative-numbered row of MATRIX. It uses Subroutine "D".

Subroutine "G" examines the negative-numbered rows of MATRIX to determine if there is an applicable substitution for the dummy variable in CHARACTER. If there is a substitution, exit is made with the row number as the value of T3; if there is no applicable substitution, an alternative exit is taken. The rows are scanned from most recent entry to oldest entry—that is, from the most negative row number to least negative.

Subroutine "H" evaluates MPFs, and is not given in detail. If the MPFs have values, they are written out with Subroutine "E". Subroutine "C" is used to deliver the objects forming the argument vector of the MPFs, and is (on exit from Subroutine "H") left prepared to deliver the first object from the current row which was not a part of the argument vector. The 3-function of Chapter 6 requires the use of Subroutine "G", which is otherwise used only once in the main flow chart.

The symbolism used in the flow charts to indicate the use of a subroutine is to enclose the letter-designation of the subroutine in a circle with a circumscribed square:

In the case of Subroutine "G", the two possible exits are distinguished: the one with a "Y" if an appropriate substitution had been found, and the other with a "N".

The Unparsing Processor Itself

A flow chart of the basic unparsing processor is given in Fig. 7.2. This flow chart contains all of the mechanism required to interpret the language of Chapter 6 with the exception of constructs contained within constructs (and, of course, the subroutines given earlier). The mechanism for constructs within constructs is given in Fig. 7.3.

The working-out of the details of Figs. 7.2 and 7.3 is left as an exercise to the reader. The fundamental process is, however, simple. The vector PARSE is used as an index to locate rows of MATRIX. Clauses cause the processing of a row to be interrupted temporarily, and the lists are used to save the pertinent values. Objects which require no interpretation (pure objects and punctuation marks) go directly to the output accretion; other symbols are interpreted.

MPFs are always evaluated immediately upon recognition. Clauses are interpreted after any phrases contained in them have been copied into MATRIX. (Clauses within phrases are copied into MATRIX un-interpreted, and are interpreted only if substitution is actually made. MPFs within phrases are interpreted before they are copied into MATRIX, and their values, if any, replace them in MATRIX.)

Figure 7.3 counts "!" to see if clauses and MPFs within braces sur-rounding constructs should, nonetheless, be interpreted. The processor is complicated by having to reconstruct the "!"s that it has counted if interpretation should not take place.

Multiple constructs, if present, are obviously processed by a com-plete reiteration of the unparsing process, with an additional test at the point shown in Fig. 7.2 to test for a 0-clause by asking if $COUNT = k$, and, if so, to start processing the construct to the left of this one rather than below it.

Some Practical Considerations

There are some modifications of both the parsing and unparsing processors which can be made to increase the efficiency of the translation process and decrease the storage required for the various tables.

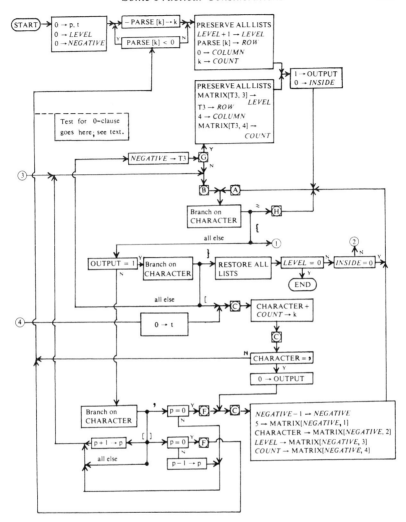

FIG. 7.2

First, it is possible to eliminate duplicate positive-numbered rows of MATRIX. This requires that the association of a construct with a rule be done by using the row number of MATRIX in which the construct appears, rather than the rule number. As an example of the savings in table space, Fig. 6.2 has 69 rules, but only 59 different constructs.

If this is done, there is then a unique designation for each unique construct. This makes possible a modification to the parsing processor so that the row corresponding to the construct "{[1]}" is never placed in the output of the parsing processor. Since this construct has no influence (in its own right) on the output accretion of the translation process, such

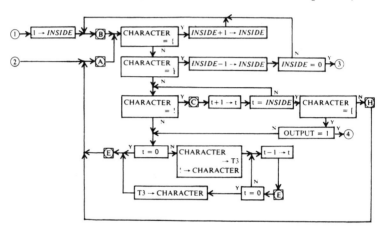

FIG. 7.3

a change reduces the size of the vector PARSE, removes yet another row from MATRIX, and reduces the number of constructs which must be processed by the unparsing processor in the course of producing the output accretion.

This requires that terminal constructs must be recognizable, perhaps by some special code following the "{".

Another modification to the unparsing processor which increases its efficiency is to attempt to write a construct into the output accretion before preserving all of the lists. In the case where a construct contains only pure objects and punctuation marks, the result is that the construct is processed without having to manipulate any of the lists at all.

The other suggestions for increasing the efficiency of the unparsing process are not easily realized in the case where multiple constructs are used, since they would result in different parsing trees for each set of constructs. In such a case, the comparison of constructs to establish construct (rather than row) numbers is made on the set of constructs associated with each rule, and only the row corresponding to the set "{[1]}...{[1]}" can be safely eliminated from the output.

CHAPTER 8

The Rest of the World

Other Metalanguages

The metasyntactic language used in this book is a recognitive form of the language originally proposed for the description of Algol [B60b]; the metasemantic and metapragmatic language is based on the first syntax-oriented translator [I61c]. There are two other types of metalanguages that have been proposed and used successfully for translator design and construction.

The first of these is a production language [F61a]. The input accretion is considered to have a pointer which indicates a single base object in the input accretion. The rules are all of the general form

If the configuration of the base objects in the input accretion surrounding the pointer is C_1, then:

(1) Change the configuration to C_2.
(2) Generate accretion A in the output accretion.
(3) Consider production P as the next production to be applied, if possible.*

The processors which have used this particular type of metalanguage tend to be translators which generate relocatable machine code, rather than an intermediate language [E64]. A mechanism for manipulating (the equivalent of) a symbol table must therefore be included in the translator processor; such a mechanism can also be included in the processor described in this book, as was mentioned in Chapter 6, by the use of an MPF which manipulates a private list.

The second type of metalanguage that has been used to specify translation processes is a language designed for the manipulation of lists (see,

* This may be constructively compared with a Turing machine [T36] [T36a].

115

among others, [M60] [N61a]). Since translators for all but the most trivial languages use lists as intermediate storage, it was felt that a language designed to express the manipulation of lists would prove useful for the specification of translator construction, and hence for the specification of a mapping from source to target language.

These approaches differ in emphasis. The list approach considers the input accretion to be a list of base objects, and manipulates it like any other list, including those used internally in the translation process. The emphasis is on the manipulation of lists (the tool), rather than on describing the grammar of the input accretion and its relationship to the target language (the task). List-manipulation languages may be quite appropriate for implementing the processors of Chapters 4 and 7.

The production approach explicitly considers the grammar of the source language and its mapping into the target language. The input accretion is considered as a suitably delimited list (say that it is delimited by the marks "⊢" and "⊣"). Each application of a production rule makes a change in the input accretion, with the ultimate goal being to reduce the accretion to "⊢ n_L ⊣", where "n_L" is the name of the source language (see Chapter 3). On the other hand, each time a rule is applied, an appropriate output is generated.

The approach described in detail in this book also requires an explicit statement of the grammar of the source language and its mapping into the target language. The significant difference between this and the production approach is that the parsing tree of the input accretion is available explicitly. This allows manipulations to be made on the tree directly; there are a number of such manipulations which may facilitate the translation from source to target language [G63a]. If the source language is a procedure-oriented language such as Algol or Fortran, and the target language is a machine-oriented language (such as an assembly language), the transformations on the parsing tree can be used to eliminate common sub-expressions, to remove redundant calculations from within loops, and to minimize the number of temporary storage locations.

Other Translators

The other metalanguages discussed in the preceding section have processors whose characteristics are determined by those metalanguages. The metalanguages used in this book, however, are susceptible of a dual interpretation. The one used in this book is known as "bottom-up", while the alternative is known as "top-down".

With the "bottom-up" technique, described in this book in detail, the parsing always has a goal in mind (either "n_L" or some subgoal), and begins the parsing towards this goal from the first unused base object of the input accretion. The parsing tree is built up in a peculiar manner: First a branch is extended downwards from the top of the tree, and then an attempt is made to forge a rule-chain towards that branch. If the "top of the tree" is understood to be the current goal, the picture of the tree as it is being constructed is a number of subtrees related only by rules of syntax which permit yet-unmade connections between them.

The parsing tree which is developed by the "top-down" approach is intuitively more satisfying. A rule is added to the subtree only when it has been shown that it applies; hence the parsing tree, although possibly incomplete, is always connected. The "top-down" method has been studied extensively [G60]. Its characteristic failing [F64c] is its inability to form parsing trees involving rule-chains which are recursive in the direction of the scan of the input accretion. That is, if the input accretion is scanned from left to right (as has been assumed throughout this book), then the single rule

$$a \quad b \quad c \quad a$$

will cause the parsing processor to continue indefinitely, as will any rule-chain in which the metaresult of the right-most rule is the same as the left metacomponent of the left-most rule.

Summary and Conclusions

The original purpose in the development of languages and their translators was to facilitate the use of a computer as a tool. Much time and more money was spent to make Language X available (and better!) on Machine Y.

The result of this proliferation and chaos was that languages for computers became the target of considerable study, in an attempt to discover simpler methods of producing translators for them.

The purpose of this book has been to present a method for minimizing the interval between the conception of a new language and its availability for use on a machine. The basic principle is to require that the specification of the language be done in a way which can be used directly by a processor to direct the translation of the language. If the specification can be used directly, then the translator is essentially complete when the specification is complete; conventionally, the completion of the specification signals the beginning of the production of the processor for the language.

The emphasis has been on generality and generalizability. Although the examples have been drawn from scientifically oriented languages, the only restrictions are those imposed by the metalanguages. The metasyntactic language allows limited context-dependence, certain classes of string-substitutions, and constraints on the endpoints of a parsing tree independent of the structure of the parsing tree as discussed in Chapters 3 and 5. The metasemantic and metapragmatic language, on the other hand, allows the inclusion of even *ad hoc* meanings, through the use of the MPFs of Chapter 6.

With any generality, there is an associated price. The translator described in this book is not as efficient as one tailored for a particular source-target language pair, but neither is it intrinsically confined to only one such pair. This freedom suggests three areas of application for a syntax-oriented translator where the generality is more important than the efficiency.

First, a language designer can use the translator as an experimental compiler. The direct use of the specification of the language to control the translation process allows a gradual growth of the language. At each phase of the growth, the utility of the language (with respect to its intended class of problems) can be assessed, and features added or deleted if appropriate. Requiring that the specifications be sufficiently accurate to allow the use of the syntax-oriented translator as an experimental embodiment guarantees that they are accurate enough to design a tailored compiler.

The second area of applicability follows from the first. Since the specification of a language in a suitable manner is tantamount to the construction of a compiler for the language, it becomes possible to allow languages to be designed somewhat more freely. Specific problem areas may have languages designed for them, rather than being constrained to use a language of broad utility but not resembling the notation of a specialized field. This tends to allow the realization of the original intent of Fortran [I54], Algol [N58] [N60] [N63], and the other higher-level languages—to permit the programming of a problem by the man with the problem, rather than the man with a knowledge of the machine.

Finally, the third area of applicability is a result of the first and second. Since the syntax-oriented translator is itself a processor, it can be described in terms of some suitable higher-level programming language. Hence, a bootstrapping technique, such as the one described in Chapter 1, is applicable to the translator itself. In an environment where machines are changing rapidly, or where specially designed computers are being manufactured, bootstrapping is the only reasonable method of providing for one machine the software that exists on another. Since one-of-a-kind machines tend to be for special areas of applicability, the generality of the syntax-oriented translator allows the development of a language suited to the same area for which the computer is designed.

A syntax-oriented translator, therefore, finds applicability in those situations where the source-target language pair cannot be held constant. In this sense, it is possible to refer to the translator as a "compiler compiler", although this description is misleading. Except for the boot-strapping case, the compiler *as such* is never compiled, but rather, the syntax-oriented translator is turned into a translator for some source-target language pair.

The requirement of compiler efficiency may be strong enough so that the syntax-oriented translator cannot be used as a production tool. Even so, there may be an advantage in using the syntax-oriented translator to design the production translator. The metalinguistic description of the mapping from source language to target language which serves to control the syntax-oriented translator can also serve as a rigorous specification for a hand-tailored translator for the particular source-target language pair. One of the earliest descriptions of the conversion from a meta-language specification to a translator [L61b] specifies the transcription of the specifications to calls on appropriate recursive subroutines. This transcription can be performed by a computer [S64] [S64a]; such a transcription processor is truly a "compiler compiler". Alternatively, a translator can be hand-coded, but the use of the metalanguage specifica-tions as a guide aids in the control of producing a processor [Y63] [Y65].

References

The following bibliography contains both the works which have been cited as references and a number of other articles which form the basis of the material in this book.

A reference consists of three or four characters. The initial majescule is the initial letter of the author's (or senior author's, or editor's, etc.) name. This is followed by two digits which are the year of publication; in some cases, the date given is the year of publication of a readily available reprint, rather than that of the original edition. When necessary, this is followed by a miniscule letter to distinguish between otherwise identical references.

BIBLIOGRAPHY

A58   Alt, F. L., "Electronic Digital Computers." Academic Press, New York and London, 1958.

A64a   American Standards Association proposed Fortran. *Comm. ACM* 7, No. 10, 590–625 (October, 1964).

B57   Backus, J. W., *et al.*, Fortran Programmer's Reference Manual. Form 32–7026–1, International Business Machines Machines, 1958.

B58   Bar-Hillel, Y., and Shamir, B., "Finite-State Languages." Hebrew Univ., Israel, 1958.

B60   Bar-Hillel, Y., Perles, A., and Shamir, E., "On Formal Properties of Simple Phrase Structure Grammars." Hebrew Univ., Israel, 1960.

B60a   Bendix G-20 Central Processor Machine Language. Form T23–1, Bendix Computer Division, Los Angeles, California, 1960.

B60b   Backus, J., The syntax and semantics of the proposed international algebraic language of the Zurich ACM-GAMM conference. *Proc. First Intern. Conf. Information Processing*, UNESCO, Paris (1960).

B62a   Bastian, A. L., Jr., A Phrase Structure Language Translator. Air Force Cambridge Res. Lab. Rept. 62-549, Cambridge, Massachusetts, 1962.

B62b   Berge, C., "The Theory of Graphs" (trans. Doig). Methuen, London, 1962. [Also published by Wiley, New York.]

B64a   Berkeley, E. C., and Bobrow, D., eds., "The Programming Language Lisp: Its Operation and Applications." Information International, Inc., Cambridge, Massachusetts, 1964.

C56   Chomsky, N., Three models for the description of language. *IRE Trans. Inform. Theory* IT-2, No. 3, 113–124 (1956).

C57a   Chomsky, N., "Syntactic Structures." Mouton & Co., 's-Gravenhage, The Netherlands, 1957. [Also published by Humanities Press, New York.]

C59a   Carr, J. W., III, Programming and coding. *In* [G59c], Vol. 2, p.2–01 ff.

C59b   Chomsky, N., On certain formal properties of grammars. *Information and Control* 2, No. 2 (1959).

C60b   Carroll, Lewis, "The Annotated Alice" (Martin Gardner, annotator). Crown (Clarkson N. Potter), New York, 1960. [The White Knight's Song is on p. 306.]

C62   Colman, H. L., and Smallwood, C., "Computer Language: An Autoinstructional Introduction to Fortran." McGraw-Hill, New York, 1962.

D61a   Dijkstra, E. W., Algol-60 Translation. Algol Bulletin Supplement No. 10, Stichting Mathematisch Centrum, Amsterdam, The Netherlands, November, 1961.

E64   Evans, A., Jr., An Algol 60 compiler. *In* "Annual Review in Automatic Programming" (R. Goodman, ed.), Vol 4. Pergamon, New York, 1964.

F61a   Floyd, R., A descriptive language for symbol manipulation. *J. Assoc. Comput. Mach.* 8, 579–584 (1961).

F62   Floyd, R. W., On the non-existence of a phrase structure grammar for Algol 60. *Comm. ACM* **5**, No. 9, 483–484 (1962).

F64   Ferguson, D. E., "A Meta-Assembly Language." Programmatics, Inc., Los Angeles, California, 1964.

F64a   Fabian, V., Structural unambiguity of formal languages. [In English.] *Czechoslovak Math. J.* **14**, No. 89, 394–430 (1964).

F64c   Floyd, R. W., The syntax of programming languages—a survey. *IEEE Trans. Electron. Computers* **13**, No. 4, 346–353 (1964).

G31   Gödel, K., Über Formal unentscheidbare Sätze der Principia Mathematica und verwandter Systeme. *Monatsh. Math. u. Phys.* **38**, 173–198 (1931).

G55   Gorn, S., An Experiment in Universal Coding. BRL Rept. 953, Aberdeen Proving Ground, Aberdeen, Maryland, 1955.

G57   Gorn, S., Standardized programming methods and universal coding. *J. Assoc. Comput. Mach.* **4**, No. 3, 254–273 (1957).

G59   Gorn, S., *et al.*, "Common Programming Language Task, Part I." Univ. of Pennsylvania, Philadelphia, Pennsylvania, 1959.

G59c   Grabbe, E. M., Ramo, S., and Wooldridge, D., "Handbook of Automation, Computation, and Control," 3 vols. Wiley, New York, 1959.

G60   Glennie, A. E., "On the Syntax Machine and the Contruction of a Universal Compiler." Carnegie Institute of Technology, Pittsburgh, Pennsylvania, 1960.

G60a   Gorn, S., and Parker, E. J., "Common Programming Language Task, Part I." Univ. of Pennsylvania, Philadelphia, Pennsylvania, 1960.

G62d   Gödel, K., "On Formally Undecidable Propositions." Basic Books, New York, 1962. [This is an English translation of [G31], with a long introduction by R. B. Braithwaite.]

G63   Greibach, S. A., Inverses of Phrase Structure Generators. Rept. NSF-11, Harvard Computation Lab., Cambridge, Massachusetts, 1963.

G63a   Garvin, L., ed., "Natural Language and the Computer." McGraw-Hill, New York, 1963.

G64   Goodman, R., ed., "Annual Review in Automatic Programming," Vol. 4. Pergamon, New York, 1964.

G65   Griffith, T. V., and Petrick, S. R., On the relative efficiencies of context-free grammar recognizers. *Comm. ACM* **8**, No. 5, 289-300 (1965).

G65a   Gallie, T. M., Jr., The Duke Algol Compiler and Syntactic Routine Method for Syntax Recognition. Final Report under Grant AF-AFOSR 62–164, Duke Univ., Durham, North Carolina, 1965.

G65b   Graham, M. L., and Ingerman, P. Z., A universal assembly mapping language. *Proc. Natl. ACM Conf.*, Cleveland, Ohio (August, 1965).

H59   Halle, M., Questions of linguistics, *Nuovo Cimento*, Suppl. **13**, No. 2, 494–517 (1959).

H60   Holt, A. W., Turanski, W. J., and Parker, E. J., "Common Programming Language Task, Part II." Univ. of Pennsylvania, Philadelphia, Pennsylvania, 1960.

H63   Holt, A. W., A Mathematical and Applied Investigation of Free Structures for Computer Syntactic Analysis. Ph.D. Dissertation, Univ. of Pennsylvania, Philadelphia, Pennsylvania, 1963.

H63a   Hamilton, D, Analysis of the Ingerman-Merner Algol Revision. ASA X3.4.2., Am. Standards Assoc., New York, 1963.

H64   Halpern, M, XPOP: A metalanguage without metaphysics. *Proc. Fall Joint Computer Conf.* 1964, Spartan Press, Washington, D.C., 1964.

I53   IBM 701 Principles of Operation. International Business Machines Form 22–6042–0, 1953.

I54   IBM preliminary report, Specifications for the IBM FORmula TRANslating System. International Business Machines, November 10, 1954. [Contains features not found in any Fortran actually released.]

I55   IBM Proposed Additions and Modifications in the Specifications for the Fortran System. International Business Machines, February 10, 1955. [Supplement to [I54].]

I57   Fortran Programmer's Primer. Form 32–0306–1, International Business Machines, 1957.

I60   IBM 7030 Reference Manual. International Business Machines Form A22–6530–1, 1960. [This may not be the same manual as the one accompanying the machine that was actually built.]

I61   IBM/SHARE S.O.S. Manual. International Business Machines, 1961.

I61a   Ingerman, P.Z., Thunks. *Comm. ACM* **4**, No. 1, 55–58 (1961).

I61b   Ingerman, P. Z., Dynamic declarations. *Comm. ACM* **4**, No. 1, 59–60 (1961).

I61c   Irons, E. T., A syntax-directed compiler for Algol 60. *Comm. ACM* **4**, No. 1 (1961).

I61d   Irons, E. T., Maintenance Manual for PSYCO—Part One. Institute for Defense Analyses, Princeton, New Jersey.

I61e   Irons, E. T., and Feurzeig, W., Comments on the implementation of recursive procedures and blocks. *Comm. ACM* **4**, No. 1, 65–69 (1961).

I62   Ingerman, P. Z., A translation technique . . . . *In* [S62a].

I62a   Iverson, K., "A Programming Language." Wiley, New York, 1962.

I63   Ingerman, P. Z., A syntax-oriented compiler . . . . Master's Thesis, Moore School of Electrical Engineering, Univ. of Pennsylvania, Philadelphia, Pennsylvania, 1963.

I63a   Ingerman, P. Z., and Merner, J., Revision of the revised Algol report. Working paper of ASA subcommittee X3.4.2. Am. Standards Assoc., New York, April 24, 1963. [Also available from author. See, in addition, [H63a].]

I64   Ingerman, P. Z., The parameterization of the translation process. *Proc. Working Conf. Formal Language Description of Languages.* North-Holland, to be published.

I66   Ingerman, P. Z., Pāṇini-Backus form suggested. *Comm. ACM* **10**, No. 3 (1967).

L53   Lerch, F. J., ORDVAC Routines for Use of IBM Input-Output Equipment. BRL Rept. 810, Aberdeen Proving Ground, Aberdeen, Maryland, 1953.

L61b   Lucas, P., The Structure of Formula-Translators. Algol Bulletin Supplement No. 16, 1961. [Available from author at IBM Laboratories in Vienna, Austria.]

L65   Lewin, R. A., A matter of syntax. *Science* **147**, No. 3656, 357ff. (Jan. 22, 1965). (Letter to the editor.)

M60   McCarthy, J., *et al.,* LISP Programmers' Manual. Computation Center, Mass. Inst. Technology, Cambridge, Massachusetts, 1960.

M61   McCracken, D. D., "A Guide to Fortran Programming." Wiley, New York, 1961.

N56 Newman, J. R., ed., "The World of Mathematics." Simon and Schuster, New York, 1956.

N56a Nagel, E., Symbolic notation, haddocks' eyes and the dog-walking ordinance. *In* "The World of Mathematics" (J. R. Newman, ed.), pp. 1878–1900. Simon and Schuster, New York, 1956.

N58 Naur, P., ed., Preliminary report—international algebraic language. *Comm. ACM* **1**, No. 12, 8–22 (1958).

N60 Naur, P., ed., Report on the algorithmic language Algol 60. *Comm. ACM* **3**, No. 5, pp. 299–314 (1960).

N60a Newell, A., *et al.*, The Elements of IPL Programming (IPL-V). Rept. P-1897, The RAND Corporation, Santa Monica, California, 1960.

N60b Newell, A., *et al.*, ed., Programmers' Reference Manual (IPL-V). Rept. P-1918, The RAND Corporation, Santa Monica, California, 1960.

N61 Naur, P., "A Course of Algol 60 Programming." Regnecentralen, Copenhagen, Denmark, 1961.

N61a Newell, A., ed., "Information Processing Language-V Manual." Prentice-Hall, Englewood Cliffs, New Jersey, 1961. [This is a commercially available reprint of [N60a] and [N60b].]

N63 Naur, P., ed., Revised report on the algorithmic language Algol 60. *Comm. ACM* **6**, No. 1, 1–17 (1963).

N63a Nagao, M., Syntactic analysis of a phrase structure language. *J. Inform. Process. Soc. Japan* **4**, No. 4, 186–193 (1963).

P37 Polya, G., Kombinatorische Anzahlbestimmungen für Gruppen, Graphen, und Chemische Verbindungen. *Acta Math.* **68**, 145–254 (1937).

P57 Perlis, A. J., Smith, J. W., and Van Zoeren, H. R., Internal Translator, (IT). A compiler for the 650 Library Program, File 2.1.001, IBM/SHARE, International Business Machines, 1957.

R53 Programming for the Univac System. Univac Form ECD19, Remington Rand, 1953.

R53a Reitweisner, G. W., The Edvac from a Programming Point of View. Branch Note No. 65, BRL Analysis and Computation Branch, Aberdeen Proving Ground, Aberdeen, Maryland, 1953.

R55 The A-2 Compiler System. Univac Form RRU-4, Remington Rand, 1955.

R56 Ravesloot, L., General Binary Card Loader PK CSB 4. Computing Bureau, International Business Machines, Poughkeepsie, New York, 1956.

R56a X-1 Assembly System. Univac Form RRU-18, Remington Rand, 1956.

R60 Math-Matic Programming, Univac Form U1568.1, Remington Rand, 1960.

R61 Rankin, B. K., III, A Programmable Grammar for a Fragment of English for Use in an Information Retrieval System. Natl. Bur. Stand. (U.S.) Rept. 7352, 1961.

R62 Rabinowitz, I. N., Report on algorithmic language FORTRAN II. *Comm. ACM* **5**, No. 6., 327–337 (1962).

R62a Sleuth II Programmer's Guide. Sperry Rand Form UP-3670, Remington Rand, 1962.

R64 Randell, B., and Russell, L.J., "Algol 60 Implementation." A.P.I.C. Studies in Data Processing No. 5. Academic Press, New York, 1964.

S61b Sammet, J. E., A definition of the Cobol 61 procedure division using Algol 60 Metalinguistics. *Proc. 16th Annual Meeting ACM*, Los Angeles, California, 1961.

S62a *Symposium on Symbolic Languages in Data Processing*. Gordon and Breach, New York, 1962.

S64 Schorre, D. V., Meta II, a syntax-oriented compiler writing language. *Proc. 19th Natl. Conf. ACM*. Assoc. for Computing Machinery, Philadelphia, Pennsylvania, 1964.

S64a Schneider, F. W., and Johnson, G. D., Meta-3, a syntax-directed compiler. Assoc. for Computing Machinery, Philadelphia, Pennsylvania, 1964.

T36 Turing, A. M., On computable numbers with an application to the Entscheidungsproblem. *Proc. London Math. Soc.* **42**, 230–265 (1937).

T36a Turing, A. M., On computable numbers with an application to the Entscheidungsproblem. A correction. *Proc. London Math. Soc.* **43**, 544–546 (1937).

W55 "Webster's New Twentieth Century Dictionary of the English Language," 2nd ed. World Publishing, New York, 1955.

W62 Warshall, S., A theorem on boolean matrices. *J. Assoc. Comput. Mach.* **9**, No. 1, 11–12 (1962).

Y61b Yershov, A. P., Kozhukhin, G. I., and Voloshin, Yu. M., Input Language for the System of Automatic Programming. Computing Center, Acad. Sci. USSR. Moscow, 1961. [In Russian. Issued as Algol Bulletin Supplement 14.]

Y63 Yershov, A. P., Kozhukhin, G. I., and Voloshin, U. M., "Input Language for Automatic Programming Systems." Academic Press, New York, 1963. [This is an updated version of [Y61b].]

Y65 Yershov, A. P., ed., "Alpha Sistemya Avtomatizatsii Programmirovaniya." Akad. Nauk SSSR, Novosibirsk, 1965.

INDEX TO REFERENCES

SUBJECT INDEX

Boldface page numbers (e.g., **47**) indicate where the indexed term is defined; these terms are italicized in the text at the point of definition. Italic page numbers (e.g., *35*) locate other places where the indexed term is italicized. Index entries in CAPITALS or *CAPITAL ITALICS* designate similar entries in the text.

Miscellaneous

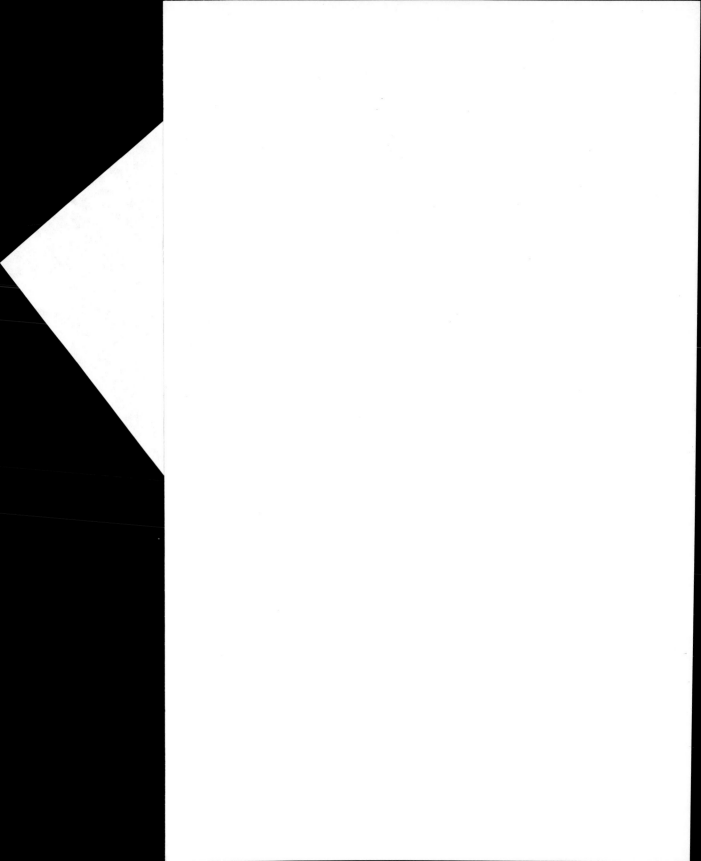

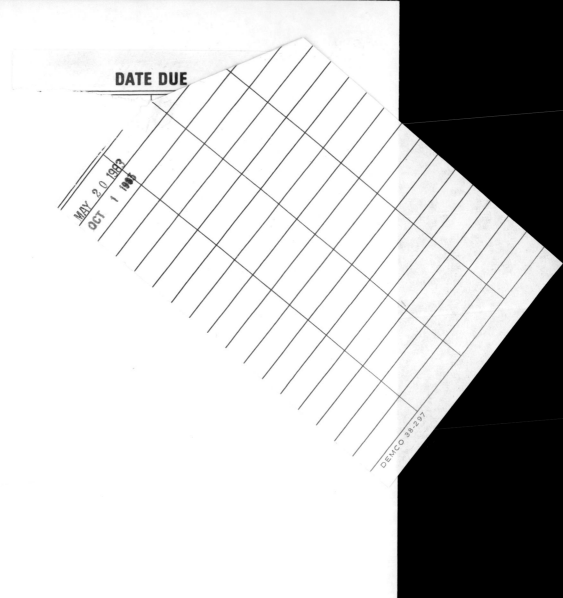

DATE DUE

MAY 2 0 1983

OCT 1 1985

DEMCO 38-297